THE QUANTUM WORLD

QUANTUM MECHANICS SIMPLIFIED

BHAVYA BANSAL

To all the physicists who inspired me to learn and write about this amazing topic.

Contents

Foreword

***"Life is strong and fragile. It's a paradox... It's both things, like quantum physics: It's a particle and a wave at the same time. It all exists all together."* ~Joan Jett**

It is indeed a proud moment for me to write a foreword for a very different kind of book that you would expect a sixteen-year-old student to the author. Bhavya Bansal's maiden book 'The Quantum World' reflects his passion to delve into the realm of the basic oneness of the universe. The subject chosen may come as a surprise for many, but for me, it is just what I would have expected from a student who makes it to the India Book of Records, for being the youngest to make a multipurpose machine that can be used in defence and industrial areas. Imagine, a thirteen-year-old being invited as a guest speaker at National Conference on Big Geospatial Data Analytics, Modelling and Application (BIGMAP) held at Punjab Remote Sensing Centre, PAU, Ludhiana. This book is a testimony of the unlimited opportunities that one has to learn and evolve.

The book provides the reader with an explanation of the origin and establishment of quantum mechanics, in a simple language. The book is a must-read not just for the students of science but for all those who wish to understand the nature of reality. The study of our subatomic parts by quantum physicists has made some HUGE discoveries about how our reality is constructed and learning about the magic of quantum physics is a worthwhile endeavour!

-Ms. Bhupinder Gogia

The Principal, Sat Paul Mittal School

The book offers a refreshing insight into Quantum Mechanics, a topic that attracts many. It's simple yet detailed text that allows everyone to better understand this aspect of physics.

Having taught him, I have come to realise his potential and enthusiasm in physics. This book has allowed him to fully boast his knowledge to the world and I hope he can continue to educate people around him.

- Ms. Madhuri Sharma

Physics Teacher, Sat Paul Mittal School

Acknowledgements

I am indebted to my pillars of strength, my parents Dr. Monika and Dr. Neeraj, for always encouraging me and supporting me in all my endeavors of life and always motivating me for exploring more and more.

I would like to acknowledge my school Sat Paul Mittal School, Ludhiana, with a motto of learning without limits, our Principal Mrs. Bhupinder Gogia, my teachers, and my friends for being the guiding spirit always.

I also acknowledge my loving younger sister, Josya for always being supportive to me.

At last, I would like to acknowledge my grandparents for their blessings and the Almighty God for showing me the right path always!

Preface

I am a 10th-grade student and like every other student, I am extremely curious to know more about the world. Some time back, I started reading about Quantum Mechanics. I have always been interested in Physics and this idea fascinated me more than ever. I decided to understand this beautiful topic and prepare a resource material that could help many more people like me.

Quantum Mechanics is considered very difficult and hard to understand by many physicists around the world. In fact, Richard Feynman, who won the Noble prize for his work on quantum electrodynamics said, "If you think you understand quantum physics, you don't understand quantum physics." However, it is arguably the most successful scientific theory in history and has helped us develop many new-generation technologies like LED screens, lasers, computers, digital cameras, nuclear power plants, and so on.

Through this book, we will take a dive into the basic concepts of Quantum Mechanics. Firstly, we must define Quantum Mechanics. The word 'Quantum' in simple terms means 'the smallest unit of something'. Quantum Mechanics, therefore, is a fundamental theory of physics that describes the physical properties of subatomic particles at a nanoscopic level. It aims to describe how all the fundamental theories of physics work on the quantum scale. It lays down the foundation of various other theories like the Quantum Field Theory and The String Theory.

The idea of Quantum Mechanics first came into existence in the early 20th century. Max Planck and Neils Bohr, two of the smartest scientists in history, are regarded as the true founders of the theory. Sir Albert Einstein, due to his efforts in this field, is sometimes regarded as the third father of Quantum Mechanics.

This reference material aims to provide authentic information about the topic using extensive details. It also aims to provide general information about Quantum Mechanics, its related theories, its applications, and many more intuitive physics concepts on the quantum scale.

CHAPTER ONE

Origin of Quantum Mechanics

1.1: CLASSICAL PHYSICS

Back in the days of the late 19th century and early 20th century, there were many new discoveries and experiments which conflicted with the model of physics known at that time. All the older theories, discovered before the quantum era, are now collectively classified as 'Classical Physics'.

1.2: PROBLEMS WITH CLASSICAL PHYSICS

During that period, due to the advancing and improving technology, there were several mysterious phenomena that pointed towards the deeper model of reality, far beyond the classical understanding of the universe known back then[1].

1.2.1: Atomic Spectra

One of the biggest mysteries in the early 1900s was the existence of "Atomic Spectra". Atomic Spectra refers to a distinct spectrum formed when specific frequencies of electromagnetic radiations are emitted or absorbed by a gas (Fig. 1.1). There was no known explanation for this phenomenon in Classical Physics.

Fig. 1.1: Diagrammatical representation of Atomic Spectra.

1.2.2: Atomic Stability

Moreover, there was a lot of confusion about the reason for the stability of an atom. According to the theories of classical physics, electrons radiate their energy and ultimately collapse into the nucleus which makes them unstable. It thus required a quantum explanation of the phenomenon to understand the true reason for the same.

1.2.3: Photoelectric Effect

Furthermore, the legendary scientist Albert Einstein proposed his theory of the Photoelectric Effect. Photoelectric Effect implied that it was possible to make electrons fly off by shining light on certain metals. It indicated to the physicists that light isn't simply a wave but a flow of particles. This was the first indication of the dual nature of quantum objects, i.e., particle-wave duality.

1.2.4: Blackbody Radiations

Another problem faced by the scientists of that time was regarding 'Blackbody Radiations'. This refers to the distribution of electromagnetic radiations of different wavelengths and frequencies which are emitted by red-hot bodies like the Sun. The Blackbody Radiation of the Sun did not match the predictions of classical physicists and therefore, became the topic of concern. Another mystery, amongst many others, was the cause of radioactivity.

1.3: SUMMARY

Therefore, it is quite evident that by the end of the 19th century, there were many loopholes in the model of physics known at that time. It was no longer possible to depend on the pre-existing theories to understand the true nature of the universe intuitively. It was time for a new revolution in the field of physics which no one could have ever imagined.

It was at this time that the idea of Quantum Mechanics was conceived. Since then, this theory has crossed all leaps and bounds to ultimately become the most successful theory of physics.

CHAPTER TWO

SUBATOMIC PARTICLES- THE STANDARD MODEL

A very interesting question about the universe that comes to mind is, what is everything around us made up of? What are the fundamental constituents of the universe? For many years, countless scientists have tried to discover the building block of everything. First, the picture converged onto a molecule. When scientists went deeper, they discovered an atom. Deeper still, they discovered the nucleus made of Protons and Neutrons around which, revolve the Electrons. But is this the answer to everything the universe is made of? Surprisingly, no. Through experiments and theories over the last centuries, everything has converged onto a single picture of the structure of matter.

The Standard Model (Fig. 2.1) is the equation of the universe. It gives the correct answer to innumerable experiments with unprecedented accuracy (Fig. 2.2). It is by any measure, one of the most successful theories of all time. This explains, block-by-block, what the world around us is made of.

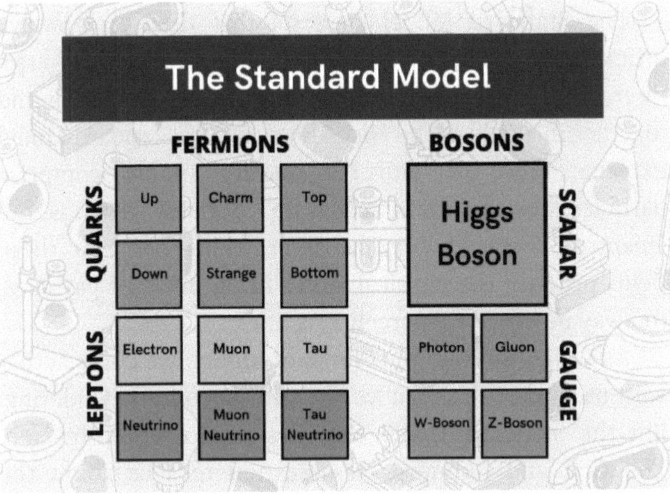

Fig. 2.1: The Standard Model of Particle Physics including two categories of particles: Fermions and Bosons.

$$Z = \int D(\text{Fields}) \exp\left(i \int d^4x \sqrt{-g} \cdot \left(R - F_{\mu\nu}F^{\mu\nu} - G_{\mu\nu}G^{\mu\nu} - W_{\mu\nu}W^{\mu\nu} + \sum_i \bar{\psi}_i \not{D} \psi_i + D_\mu H^\dagger D^\mu H - V(H) - \lambda_{ij} \bar{\psi}_i H \psi_j\right)\right)$$

Fig. 2.2: The Equation of the universe. This equation is the mathematical representation of the Standard Model.

2.1: PARTICLES OF THE STANDARD MODEL

The Standard Model suggests that there are twelve different types of matter particles in the universe, interacting with three forces, and everything is bound together in a field of the Higgs Bosons. The Standard Model explains how the universe doesn't simply comprise particles, instead, it is made up of fields. This is the Quantum Field Theory.The interactions between these fields produce the physical world in the form of particles, the way in which we perceive reality.

As we go through the Standard Model, we come across various names that can very easily become bewildering. But the Standard Model classifies particles step-by-step. The first and foremost classification tells us about the nature of the particle. A particle is either a **Fermion**, a matter particle, or a **Boson**, a force particle[2]. Fermions are the building blocks of matter, like those comprising an atom. Bosons, on the other hand, are force particles, responsible for all the interactions between Fermions.

There is a certain characteristic of Fermions that distinguishes them from Bosons. Fermions obey the **Pauli Exclusion Principle**. This principle states that not more than two Fermions of the same type can occupy the same energy level in a quantum system. Bosons, however, due not obey this principle. Instead, they do quite opposite than that. They usually try to occupy the lowest energy level in a quantum system because theoretically, infinitely many Bosons can pile over each other without violating any law.

2.1.1: Fermions

Everything we are composed of can be reduced to just three types of matter particles, the **Electron**, and the two primary types of **Quarks** called the Up-Quark and the Down-Quark. These three are the most important Fermions.

The Up Quarks carry a charge of +2/3 and Down Quarks carry the charge of -1/3. The more familiar matter particle Proton is composed of two Up-Quarks and one Down-Quark, while the Neutrons are composed of Two Down-Quarks and One Up-Quark. So, a Proton has an overall 1-unit positive charge, and Neutrons are neutral.

Protons and Neutrons together make the nucleus of the atom. Electrons, the third type of Fermions, revolve around the nucleus in specific energy levels. This completes the model of an atom.

The fourth type of matter particle is called **Neutrino**, and it is quite different from other particles. Neutrinos are extremely light, a-millionth of the mass of an electron, and they do not interact with anything around. There are trillions of Neutrinos reaching the Earth from the Sun and other heavenly bodies daily. Every second, millions of Neutrinos pass through your body[3].

So, we know the four principal Fermions, the Electron, Up-Quark, Down-Quark, and the Neutrino. The other eight particles are nothing but generations of each of the four Fermions.

The Standard Model predicts three different versions of Electrons. One is simply the Electron, and the others are **Muon** and **Tau**. Both Muon and Tau particles have all properties the same as an Electron, but with a different mass. Muon weighs about 200 times the mass of an Electron while Tau weighs about 3000 times more. Like electrons, the neutrinos are known as the **Electron Neutrino**, the

Muon Neutrino, and the **Tau Neutrino**. The electrons and neutrinos are collectively called **Leptons**.

Similarly, there are two heavier versions of the Up-Quark, called **Charm-Quark**and **Top-Quark** (heaviest Up-Quark), and two heavier versions of the Down-Quarks, the **Strange-Quark**, and the **Bottom-Quark** (heaviest Down-Quark). These six particles are collectively termed **Quarks**.

The second and third-generation particles are extremely rare. They are generally not observed, and once created are very unstable and decay to the first-generation particles. But these particles can be detected in particle accelerators, so we know that they do exist. Also, these 12 particles are necessarily characterized as Fermions because all of them can be described by a single equation called **the Dirac Equation**, written by Sir Paul Dirac (Fig. 2.3).

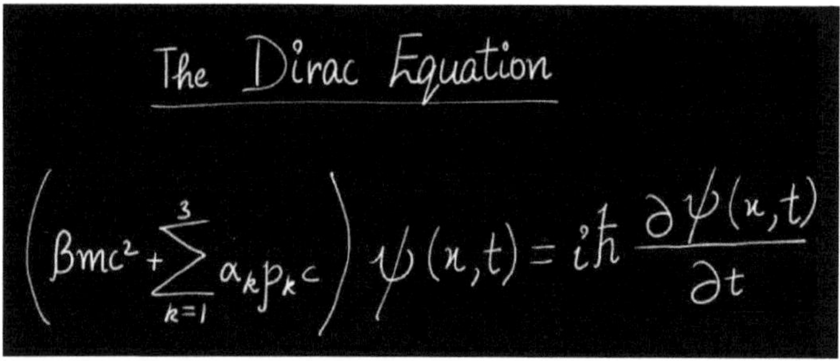

Fig. 2.3: The Dirac Equation derived by Sir Paul Dirac. The equation mathematically describes the symmetry between different Fermions.

The Standard Model explains why Fermions exist in a set of four and not any other number. The equations of the Standard Model bind the particles of all the four types to exist simultaneously. There is a mathematical condition that proves to us that if we have one kind of particle, the other three must exist as well. However, the reasons for the existence of specifically three generations are not well understood.

2.1.2: Bosons

The Bosons form the other half of the Standard Model. These are force particles, responsible for all inter-fermion interactions. The Standard Model predicts three main forces in the universe, the **Electromagnetic Force**, the **Strong Force**, and the **Weak Force**. With each of these forces, there is an associated particle, called a Boson. We can consider that Fermions are continuously swapping Bosons between them which affects their momentum and ultimately develops forces between them.

The most familiar force is Electromagnetism, and the particle associated with it is the **Photon**. The electromagnetic force is responsible for various chemical processes and has been utilized for the creation of most modern technology. The force acts only on certain types of fermions. This is because Photons interact only with certain particles, only those particles which possess electric charge. This includes all the quarks and electrons, but not neutrinos. Neutrinos are the only Fermions that are isolated to the electromagnetic force.

The next force is the strongest force known and is appropriately called the Strong Force. This force acts only on Quarks, and therefore, subsequently on Protons and Neutrons. This is the force that holds the Quarks together in a Proton and a Neutron and holds protons and neutrons together in the nucleus of an atom. The particle of Strong Force is called **Gluon**. The Strong Force produces a field unlike the field of Electromagnetism, it produces a flux tube, which ends only when it finds another quark. This is what makes the Strong Force strong. This is also the reason why we never see Quarks alone.

The third type of force is the Weak Force. It acts only on subatomic particles, and instead of binding particles together, this force results in the decay of particles. Due to the Weak Force, all the higher generations of Fermions, like Muon, Strange Quark, Tau Neutrino, etc., decay into their first-generation particles.

This force allows a Down-Quark to become an Up-Quark by releasing an electron and a neutrino. This phenomenon is called Radioactive Beta-Decay. In this way, Weak force is responsible for Nuclear Fusion reactions that power the Sun and produce the energy required for life on Earth.

According to the Standard Model, the Weak Force is represented by two different particles: The **W-Boson** and the **Z-Boson**. Weak Force is the only force, which is experienced by all Fermions, which means that neutrinos interact only with Weak Force particles.

2.1.3: The Higgs Boson

The Standard Model predicts the existence of another particle, which is neither a matter particle nor a force particle. It is, however, the most essential component of the Standard Model, and it keeps the theory unified. This is the **Higgs Boson**. It is not appropriate to refer to Higgs Boson as a particle, it is a field. The Higgs field is an infinite field that interacts with all particles. This interaction is essential because it is due to this interaction that particles have mass. Photons, the particles of the electromagnetic force, do not interact with the Higgs Field, and therefore, they have no mass and can travel with the speed of light, the maximum possible speed allowed by the laws of the universe itself. In the absence of the Higgs Field, all particles would be flying around in the universe at the speed of light. This is what makes the Higgs Boson so important.

2.2: PROBLEMS WITH THE STANDARD MODEL

It is quite evident that the Standard Model of particle physics explains everything. It explains the building blocks of matter, the different interactions between them, and the subsequent forces acting between them. However, there is one force that is unaccounted for. It is the force of Gravity. Although the Theory of Relativity explains the force of Gravity in detail, it is somehow not possible to incorporate Gravity into quantum mechanics.

This is mainly because General Relativity is a theory of classical mechanics based on classical physics, while Quantum Mechanics deals only with quantum objects. Moreover, the force of gravity is so weak on the quantum level that it has a negligible effect on other particles.

Quantum Mechanics doesn't predict the existence of a Graviton, the particle of gravity. Therefore, scientists have come up with fascinating theories to describe Quantum Gravity, like The String Theory and Quantum Loop Gravity. However, none of them have the experimental verifications to support them and have issues of their own.

Many more things are missing here, like realms of Dark Matter and Dark Energy, which comprise a whopping 95% of the universe.

Other questions like why neutrinos are a million times are lighter than electrons, why are Muon and Tau electrons as heavy as they are, and why is there no possible way to predict their masses without directly measuring them. But there is some pattern, indicating that there is some underlying structure that is still waiting to be uncovered.

2.3: DEEPER LOOK AT THE STANDARD MODEL

So, this is the Standard Model, twelve matter particles called Fermions, three Forces having four particles called Bosons, and the most important particle, the Higgs Boson.

For now, the Standard Model is too successful, giving the right answer to each and every experiment being conducted. However, in the hope of knowing what lies beyond, scientists look to find experiments to which the Standard Model answers wrong. And there is a possible hint for the same, according to the **Grand Unified Theory**, which states that the Gluon, W Boson, and Z Boson are not different, but simply manifestations of the same force. However, there is no experimental confirmation for the same yet.

This isn't the end of the Standard Model just yet. The first look at the Standard Model can be highly misleading. The theory of Special Relativity implies certain restrictions on the universe. There are certain symmetries of the universe that the Standard Model must abide by. Therefore, there is a need to have a deeper understanding of the Standard Model.

The particles of the Standard Model possess certain properties, based on which it is possible to differentiate them. One of the most important of them is Spin. It is imperative to understand Spin beforehand to be able to relate different ideas of Quantum Mechanics.

2.4: QUANTUM SPIN

There are different types of momenta possessed by an object based on its direction of motion. Two of the most common ones are Linear Momentum and Angular Momentum. When an object traces a straight trajectory, it has Linear Momentum, and when the object traces a curved trajectory, it has Angular Momentum. Quantum Spin is a type of Angular Momentum possessed by all quantum objects, and it differentiates particles of different kinds.

However, spin doesn't simply mean the momentum due to the rotation of particles about its axis. Quantum Spin refers to the **Inherent Angular Momentum**. According to Quantum Mechanics, even stationary quantum objects have some angular momentum which is an in-built property of all quantum objects. The spin of particles is extremely important to understand because it is associated with the behavior of particles in different environments, like electric and magnetic fields.

Momentum is a vector quantity. To describe the momentum of a particle, we must describe its magnitude as well as the direction of motion. The slight differences in the momentum of particles result in variations between particles of the same family.

2.4.1: Effect of Direction of Measurement on Spin

Electrons are the best particles to explain this property. They have two types of possible spins based on their direction, Spin-Up or Spin-Down. Electrons' inherent linear momentum makes them appear to be spinning clockwise or counterclockwise. Spin-Up means clockwise motion, while Spin-Down means counterclockwise motion. Spin is a weird phenomenon because the spin of any particle is never certain whenever measured in a particular direction.

When an electron is measured for spin vertically, its superposition collapses and it takes up either Spin-up or Spin-Down. Now if the same electron is measured for its spin horizontally, either left or right, it takes either Spin-Left or Spin-Right but loses its identity as Spin-Up or Spin-Down particle. If you then again measure the electron vertically, 50% of particles will not be in their original condition of Spin-up or Spin-Down. It is strictly impossible to be certain of the spin of the electron in the direction perpendicular to the direction of the original measurement because it has an equal probability of being Spin-Up or Spin-Down. This is the Heisenberg Uncertainty Principle.

2.4.2: Magnitude of Intrinsic Angular Momentum

The Quantum Spin of particles follows a very strange property which is described by the momentum of particles. According to Quantum Mechanics, Quantum Spin is quantized. The magnitude of Spin of all particles of a family, like Fermions, is constant.

The magnitude of Spin of a particle is described either by an integer, like 1, or by a half-integer, like ½. This value is the multiple of the Reduced Planck's Constant (1.0545 * 10^{-34}), named after Max Planck, the father of Quantum Mechanics.

There is symmetry in the Standard Model which unifies different particles together, The Pauli Exclusion Principle. The basis of this principle is Quantum Spin. All Fermions behave according to the Pauli Exclusion Principle because they have half-integer spin, like the Electron which has Spin-½. All Bosons, on the other hand, are integer spin particles, like a Photon that has Spin-1. The Higgs Boson, the special particle of Quantum Mechanics, is the only particle with Spin-0.

Particles can have different magnitudes of spin. For example, an electron can have Spin +½ or Spin -½. Photons, on the other hand, can have Spin +1 and Spin -1. This is the nature of all Quantum Objects. But the Inherent Angular Momentum of a particle can never be 0 because it will go against the Heisenberg Uncertainty Principle, the basis of Quantum Mechanics.

This is the general idea about particle spin, and what it means to measure particle spin. Spin, more accurately, should be described as the Intrinsic Angular Momentum of a quantum object. However, for simplicity, the term 'Spin' works well.

2.5: Handedness of Particles

The direction of Spin of a particle with respect to its direction of motion determines the handedness of particles. If the particle's motion is in the direction of its spin, it is called a Right-Handed particle, and if it moves in the direction opposite to its spin, it is called a Left-Handed particle. This is the basic principle of 'Handedness of Particles'.

This property is extremely important in Quantum Mechanics. It plays a key role in the way different particles interact with the world.

2.6: QUARKS

2.6.1: Charged Weak Interactions

All quarks exist both as right-handed and left-handed. Upon interaction with the Weak Force, the left-handed Down-Quarks can become left-handed Up-Quarks. This phenomenon is observed upon interactions with W-Bosons. The W-Bosons, themselves, are of two different types, **W^+ Boson** and **W^- Boson**. Such interaction of quarks is called "Charged Weak Interaction" [4].

However, for some unknown reason, this doesn't happen with Right-handed Quarks. The right-handed quarks always retain their identity and never participate in Charged Weak Interactions. This phenomenon suggests the importance of handedness of particles in Quantum Mechanics.

2.6.2: Color Charge

Quarks are special matter particles, and therefore, have strange properties of their own. They not only possess an electric charge, but also a color charge. This property of

Quarks is heavily linked with Special Relativity, which imposes some restrictions on the nature of quantum objects.

The quarks can have three different color charges, **red**, **green**, and **blue**. Since quarks also have handedness, there are six sub-classifications of each of the six quarks. E.g., a Left-handed Red Charm-Quark or a Right-handed Green Bottom-Quark. There are some restrictions on color charges and handedness of different quarks inside a proton or a neutron. Quantum Mechanics states that all quarks in a proton or a neutron must have the same handedness, and all of them must have different color charges.

The color charge of particles is extremely important. This is because, it enables quarks to interact with the particles Strong Force, the Gluons. Gluons have a special property that they only interact with quarks of different color charges. Since the three combining quarks are of different color charges, a neutral or colorless charge is formed, which enables us to see these particles. This color charge is the reason why individual quarks cannot be observed.

This property of the Strong Force applies to both left-handed and right-handed quarks. This means that three right-handed quarks combine the same way as the left-handed quarks to form Protons and Neutrons. But both left-handed and right-handed quarks do not exist together in a Proton or a Neutron. This also implies that only left-handed neutrons can change into protons by Charged Weak Interactions, but not the right-handed neutrons.

To observe a particle, an overall colorless charge is required. This can either be attained by three different quarks, as in a proton or by a Quark and an **Anti-Quark**, as in a **Meson**. Yes, there are Anti-Quarks for each type of quark, with color charges as Anti-Red, Anti-Blue, and Anti-Green.

2.7: Leptons

Leptons form the other half of the Fermions. Leptons include electrons and neutrinos. The rules applying to left-handed quarks also apply to left-handed neutrinos. A left-handed neutrino can also change into a left-handed electron and vice versa, using Charged Weak Interactions with the exchange of W^+ and W^- Bosons, like that in quarks.

Just like quarks, both left-handed and right-handed electrons exist, but strangely, neutrinos are only left-handed. Right-handed neutrinos have never been detected even after innumerous experiments.

Leptons do not possess a color charge like quarks. They are colorless and therefore, can be observed individually. However, just like anti-quarks, anti-leptons also exist, one for each type of lepton.

It must be noted that anti-particles are not only opposite in color charge, but also electric charge and handedness. For example, the anti-particle of a left-handed electron has a charge of +1 and is called a right-handed **Positron**. Since right-handed neutrinos do not exist, left-handed anti-neutrinos also do not exist.

The Standard Model represents all these particles with just 12 Fermions to prevent the perplexity of the Standard Model. Moreover, all the sub-classifications have basic similar properties like mass and electric charge, therefore, they are not regarded as different particles altogether but as variations of the same particles (Fig. 2.4).

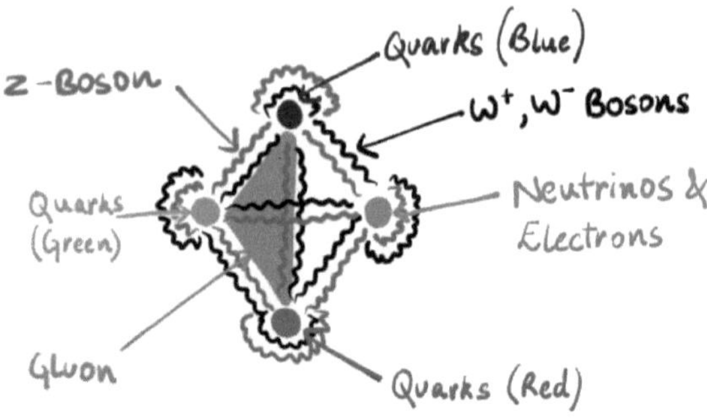

Fig. 2.4: Diagrammatical representation of the interactions between Fermions and Bosons.

2.8: Bosons

Bosons are particles that represent different forces in the universe. The particles of Electromagnetic force are called Photons. The nature and properties of all photons are the same, and therefore, do not have any sub-classifications.

Now moving on to the Strong Force. Gluons, the particles of the Strong Force, mediate the interactions between the quarks. Since quarks have a color charge, gluons also have color charges. Based on their color charge, gluons are of eight different types. Theoretically, all the eight types of gluons can combine to form a colorless Glue-ball which should be observable, but this phenomenon has never been observed.

The Bosons of the Weak Force include two W Bosons, W^+ and W^- Bosons, and one Z Boson. This force is responsible for the Charged Weak Interactions. Z-Boson doesn't possess an electric charge, and therefore, mediates the transfer of momentum, Spin, and energy.

This was the list of all Fermions and Bosons in the known universe. All these particles are unified by special particles in the universe, the Higgs Boson discussed before.

CHAPTER THREE

Quantum Leap

Quantum Leap is a strange but fundamental phenomenon of Quantum Mechanics discovered by Sir Neils Bohr. Quantum Leap refers to the irregular, random, and instantaneous transition of an electron from one energy shell to another in an atom (Fig. 3.1).

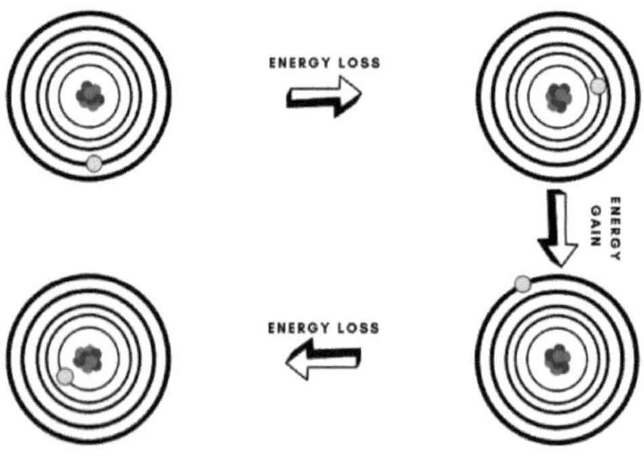

Fig. 3.1: Quantum Leap.

The leap of an electron can be to a lower energy level or a higher energy level. Whenever an electron gains a discrete quantity of energy, it leaps to a higher energy level in the quantum system. When the electron radiates the energy, it leaps to a lower energy level in the system. According to Quantum Mechanics, there is no in-between stage of a quantum leap, which means that Quantum Leap is instantaneous. Quantum Leap can be described as an irregular phenomenon based on uncertainty and chance in which electrons gain or lose energy and jump into higher or lower energy levels. This jump is instantaneous and random[5].

The electron leaps at random, following strict rules of probability. The discrete indivisible units of energy released or gained by the electron are called **Quanta**. The energy absorbed or released is a whole number multiple of quanta. Therefore, it is possible to predict the location of electrons and define the areas where the electron can never be after the leap. The electron is expected to be in some place and not to be in another upon absorption or radiation of energy, simply because the energy change occurs in a discrete number of Quanta.

Quantum Leap is the possible reason for the occurrence of Atomic Spectra. Whenever a particle releases or absorbs energy in discrete units, the energy could be seen in the form of distinct colored light rays in a prism.

CHAPTER FOUR

WAVE-PARTICLE DUALITY AND DOUBLE-SLIT EXPERIMENT

The double-slit experiment is one of the most impressive experiments ever conceived. This experiment, in all its different forms, clearly indicates how wonderfully weird the Quantum World is! This was the first experiment that showcased the true nature of a subatomic particle, quantum objects show characteristics of both particles and waves at the same time i.e., **Wave-Particle Duality**. This underlines the true nature of the Quantum world based on uncertainty and probability.

This experiment was first performed by Thomas Young in 1801 to prove that light propagates in the form of a wave. For the same reason, the double-slit experiment is also referred to as Young's experiment[6].

4.1: EXPERIMENTAL SETUP

In the double-slit experiment, a gun capable of throwing electrons is fixed horizontally. Two slits are cut out from cardboard, and the cardboard is placed vertically in front of the gun such that it allows the electrons to pass only through the two slits. An aluminum sheet is placed vertically behind the cardboard such that electrons are incident on it (Fig. 4.1).

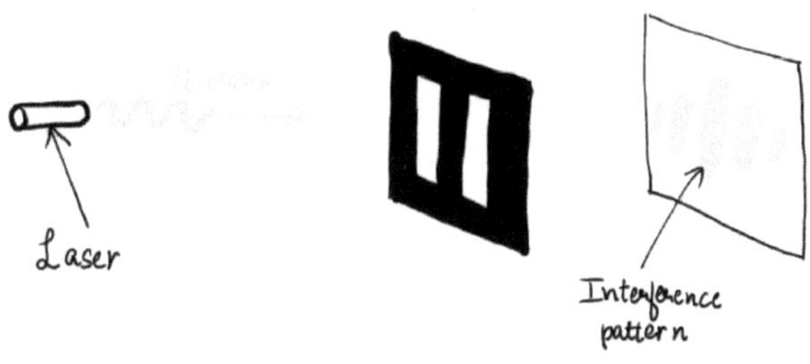

Fig. 4.1: The experimental setup of the Double-Slit Experiment. An interference pattern is observed on the screen, following the strict rules of probability.

4.2: OBSERVATIONS

The expected observation was that two columns of electrons would be incident on the sheet, corresponding to the two slits. However, that is not the case. What we see is an interference pattern that initially seems to go against the logic of classical physics.

While traveling through the medium, the electrons travel as waves (Fig. 4.2). Upon reaching the cardboard, two new waves arise from the respective slits which lead to the formation of new peaks and troughs in the medium. In the region where two peaks meet, a higher peak is formed;

where two troughs meet, a higher trough is formed; and when a peak meets a trough, they cancel each other out. This highlights the reason why distinct interference patterns are formed. A similar interference pattern is obtained when photons are used instead of electrons.

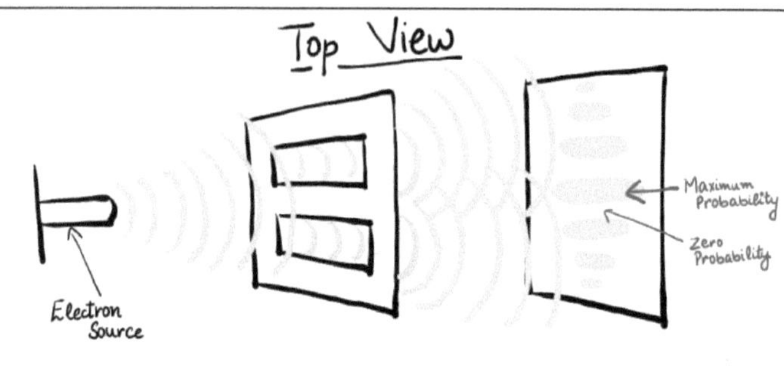

Fig. 4.2: Highly diagrammatic representation of Double-Slit Experiment. The waves symbolize Wave-Particle Duality.

But here a question arises, how does a single particle, like an electron, forms separate waves and interacts with itself to form an interference pattern? The explanation for this is wave-particle duality. Electrons individually act as waves and therefore can interact with themselves. But it is important to understand that the wave is not a physical wave but is the mathematical description of the particle's motion, used to calculate its position or momentum. A wave of a quantum object is a set of probabilities that tells us how likely an electron exists in a particular position. This is done using the **Born Rule**.

However, a quantum wave cannot be observed. An electron is only observed as a particle, not a wave. In fact, a quantum object shows a wave-like behavior only until an observation is made. Observation, in this case, means any kind of interaction with the real world. This has been proven by various experiments.

The scientists, to study the nature of the particle of the wave, placed detectors in front of the slits to measure the phenomenon. However, whenever they turned on the detectors, the particles stopped behaving like a wave and no interference pattern was formed. Only two columns of electrons were seen corresponding to the two slits.

The scientists even tried to place the detector behind the slits. The reason why they decided to do so was that as the electron would have passed the slits, the electron would have already formed separate waves behind the slits as it was not measured earlier. However, the same result was obtained since the electrons somehow already knew about the existence of detectors behind the slits. But on turning the detectors off, an interference pattern was formed.

The scientists then decided to outsmart the electrons by turning on the detectors once some of the electrons had already passed. However, this ideology somehow also failed, as somehow the electrons knew that the scientists were going to turn on the detectors after a while. Such a result was quite shocking and unexplainable. This insisted to the scientists that once they turned on the detectors, the electrons traveled back in time and formed no interference pattern.

But one thing quite certain after all the experiments were that the wave function of the particle always collapses, and the particle takes up a definite position on screen upon observation by a detector as it no longer exhibits the properties of a wave[7].

For this reason, it is quite difficult to study and formalize this concept. But how does the wave collapse into a particle upon measurement? How does the wave in the quantum world change into a particle in reality? Sadly, nobody has been able to concretely justify this phenomenon. Many scientists have tried to come up with interesting theories about reality to justify this, including 'Many Worlds' theory, Copenhagen theory, QBISM, and many more but this still requires a lot of further research.

4.3: SUPERPOSITION

Scientists might not have figured out how the conversion from a wave to a particle takes place, but they have been able to figure out how the quantum object behaves like a wave. This behavior is explained by the **Superposition Principle**. This principle is awfully strange because it isn't something one can observe in their daily life.

According to the superposition principle, when a particle is not being measured, it exists in all the different positions it can possibly be in, at the same time. However, once you turn on the detector to measure the particle, the wave function collapses, and the particle takes up any one of the positions based on the probability distribution calculated using the Born Rule. The superposition can basically be understood as: things could be at two or more places at a time.

4.3.1: Schrödinger's Cat

Schrödinger explained the Superposition principle by an experiment called the Schrödinger's cat. In this experiment, Schrödinger imagined placing his cat inside a sound-proof opaque box having a radioactive sample (Fig. 4.3). The Radioactive sample had a 50% chance of killing the cat. But as the box is covered, we have no idea whether the cat is dead or alive. We can know about the condition of the cat only when we open the box.

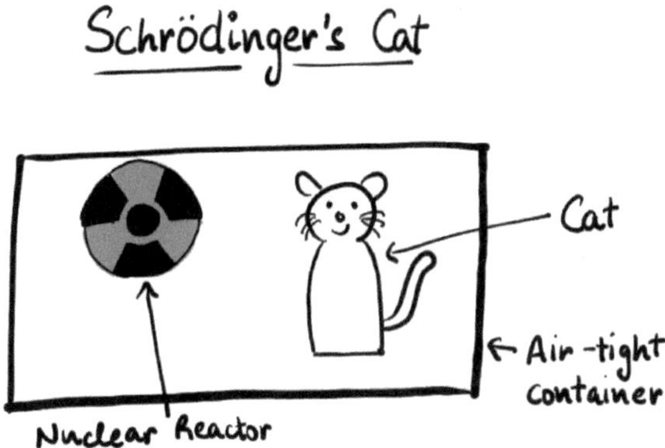

Fig. 4.3: Schrödinger's Cat. The cat is said to be in a superposition of being dead and alive at the same time.

So, if the cat was like an electron, using the superposition principle, we can say that once the box is closed, the cat is in superposition, that the cat is dead and alive at the same time, and when we measure it, which here means opening the box, then the superposition of the cat collapses and we will know whether the cat is alive or dead.

Although the analogy might seem incorrect to some because it is impossible for the cat to be dead and alive at the same time, the main objective of the experiment was to explain the superposition principle. This experiment also indicates how peculiar the laws of quantum mechanics are when it comes to explaining the behavior of particles.

CHAPTER FIVE

WAVE FUNCTION

The motion of subatomic particles is described in the form of a wave. As described in the double-slit experiment, the subatomic particles independently exist in the form of waves, and not particles. The wave function of the Quantum Particle is explained by **Schrödinger's Wave Equation** (Fig. 5.1).

$$i\hbar \frac{\partial}{\partial t}\psi(r,t) = -\frac{\hbar^2}{2m}\nabla^2\psi(r,t) + V(r,t)\psi(r,t)$$

where,

i = imaginary number $(\sqrt{-1})$

$\hbar = 1.05459 \times 10^{-32}$

ψ = wave-function

∇^2 = Laplacian Operator

Fig. 5.1: Schrödinger Wave Equation.

5.1: THE BORN RULE

Although we can never see a wave function due to the collapse of wave function upon measurement, what we can do with is wave function is to predict the likeliness of the particle to be at a place. This is done by the **'Born Rule'** which gives us a probability distribution of the possible locations of particles (Fig. 5.2). So, Quantum Mechanics implies that the universe is probabilistic and uncertain. We can't exactly know with absolute certainty where the particle will turn up, the best we have is a probability distribution[1].

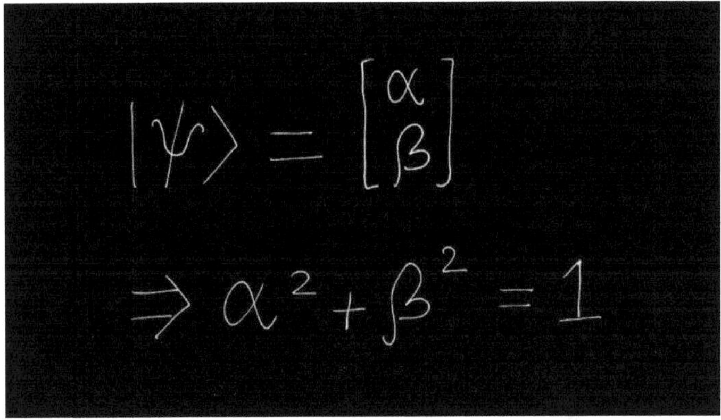

Fig. 5.2: The Born Rule. *Alpha* and *Beta* represent State Vectors of the two possible states, say, Spin-Up and Spin-Down.

For example, if the quantum object can only be two possible states, like Spin-Up or Spin-Down, then the probability of it being in either of the states is calculated using the state vectors (SV) of the two states. The Born Rule says,

$$(SV_{\text{Spin-Up}})^2 + (SV_{\text{Spin-Down}})^2 = 1$$

Similarly, for the calculation of the position of a particle from its wavefunction, we take the amplitude of the wave (State Vectors) and square it, so all the negative values also become positive, and we, therefore, get the probability distribution of the wave. The global maxima will have the highest probability of finding the particle at that place, while the global minima will have the least probability (Fig. 5.3).

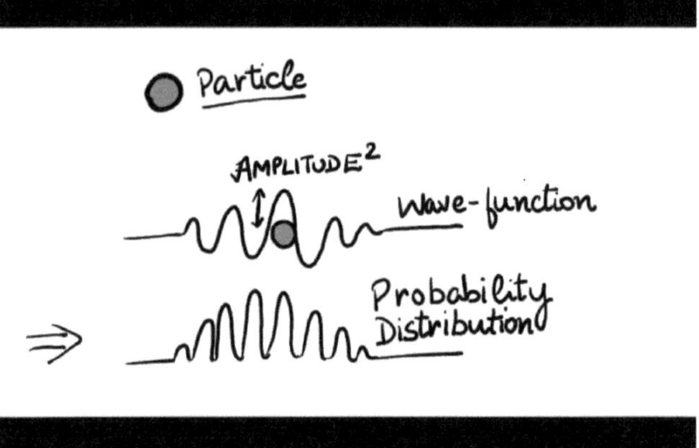

Fig. 5.3: Diagrammatic representation of Probability Distribution graph from wave-function.

5.2: SUMMARY

All this, once again, indicates to us that the Universe is full of uncertainty and probability which also goes against the laws of classical physics. This also goes against the belief of Sir Albert Einstein, who believed that everything in the world is absolute and certain. However, the success of this theory experimentally and mathematically has certainly proved the validity of the theory of Quantum Mechanics.

We must consider one more thing in relation to this fact. We know that particles behave like waves. So why is it that individuals like humans or larger matter don't behave the same way? The reason for this, according to Quantum Mechanics, is that the wavelength of the object decreases with an increase in the size of the object. So, at the size of humans, it is impossible to detect the wave-like behavior because the wave is smaller than the smallest length that can be measured (Planck's length).

But here a problem arises. No one has seen a wave, and according to the current theory, no one can ever see it. The wave is just a mathematical expression of the behavior of particles. We don't have any physics to describe how the wave collapses into a particle, and this is a gap in our knowledge that needs to be filled.

CHAPTER SIX

Quantum Entanglement

Quantum Entanglement is arguably one of the most bizarre concepts in physics. Quantum Entanglement tells us about the interlinking of properties of two particles upon a special interaction. The two particles get interlinked over space in a way that if the property of one particle is changed, an instantaneous impact of this is observed on the other particle no matter how far the particle may be (Fig. 6.1).

ENTANGLEMENT

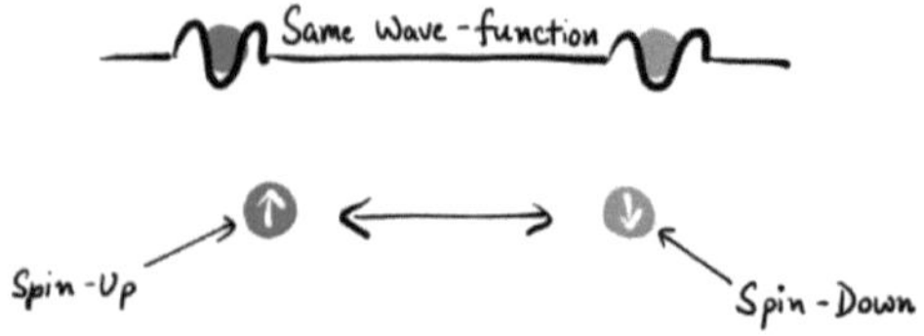

Fig. 6.1: Quantum Entanglement. The entangled particles show opposite particle-spin even when light-years apart.

The theory tells us that both particles can be mathematically described using a single wave function, meaning the particles are entangled. The properties of both particles become interdependent. But such an idea was absurd for many scientists because it implied that entangled particles could communicate instantaneously even if they are light-years away from each other, which was against Einstein's Theory of Relativity which doesn't allow anything to travel faster than light. He called such results "Spooky action at a distance" [8]. However, quantum entanglement is an experimentally proven fact.

6.1: ENTANGLEMENT AND SPIN

Quantum Entanglement can be better understood using Quantum Spin. When an electron is measured for its spin, it could either be a Spin-Up electron, or a Spin-Down electron. But what if the particle has a vertical spin and measurement is done horizontally? In such a situation, the particle has a 50-50 chance of being Spin-Up or Spin-Down. Since Quantum Spin is an inherent property, the particle will always retain its spin. This means that the act of measurement alters the spin of a particle.

The probability of the spin, where A is the angle between the initial spin of particle and direction of measurement of Spin, is determined by the formula:

$P(\text{Spin}) = \text{Cos}\,(\frac{1}{2} \cdot A)^2$

This is also explained using superposition. The electrons are in the superposition of being both Spin-Up and Spin-Down at the same time. Once the particle is measured, its superposition collapses and it takes up either Spin-Up or Spin-Down.

If we measure the spin of two entangled particles in the same direction, both always show the opposite spin. In case one of the particles shows Spin-Up, the other particle must show Spin-Down. This process is instantaneous and works even in case the measurement is perpendicular to the direction of spin. This phenomenon occurs due to the Law of Conservation of Linear Momentum which compels the second particle to take up the spin opposite to that of the first one. The particles don't have a definite Intrinsic Angular Momentum, it is only upon measurement that the particles take up a definite spin.

Some theorists interpret this result as the instantaneous communication between the entangled electrons even over light-years, and one's measurement influences the other faster than the speed of light. But this didn't go too well with Einstein. He proposed another explanation that upon entanglement, the electrons contain hidden information with the help of which they would choose their spin in a particular direction and that there was no communication between the entangled particles.

To test which of the two interpretations was right, John Bell designed a famous experiment. The experimental observation proved that the electrons do not contain hidden information, and even if they do, they update their information when either of the particles is measured, instantaneously. But such an experiment doesn't rule out the Theory of Relativity because it is not possible to do communication using entangled particles as the results obtained are random[8].

The theory of entanglement again arises hundreds of questions that are unanswered to date and the statement

"Spooky action at a distance" is justified.

6.2: TELEPORTATION

Quantum Entanglement makes the fictional idea of **Teleportation** possible. But not the teleportation of humans, certainly. Teleportation of subatomic particles is possible and has also been performed.

This is done by keeping one of the entangled particles in one observatory, and the second in another observatory to which it is to be teleported. When the particle to be teleported is made to interact with one of the entangled particles, the definite properties of the particle are studied and passed on to the entangled particle far away with the use of entanglement. As a result, the original particle degenerates, and its identical copy is formed. This identical copy is none other than the entangled electron.

One might imagine that it is just a copy, but no, that particle exhibits all the same properties, and it seems as if the particle has been teleported.

Imagine teleportation of humans by this process though. If possible, an identical copy of a human being can be formed at another place, in which all the particles have the same properties as the original one. However, is it possible to do it? It is possible but the amount of computational power needed to teleport around 10^{29}particles of the human body will take more than a trillion years to teleport. It is an interesting sector of further research, even though we are far from making teleportation possible right now.

CHAPTER SEVEN

QUANTUM TUNNELLING

Theory of Quantum Tunnelling, strangely enough, allows quantum objects to pass straight through a wall, provided the wall is finite. Although the probability of this happening to a macro-object like a human being is too small to occur, the probability increases continuously as the size of the object decreases. At the size of an electron, it is even possible for it to tunnel through a barrier all the time.

In the chapter Wave-Function, we learnt that particles behave like waves and their position can be described using their wave function. The wave-function of a wave is said to decrease exponentially through a barrier, but never end completely if the barrier is finite (Fig. 7.1). It is even possible for an electron in a laboratory to tunnel and reach Mars, although the probability for the same is very low.

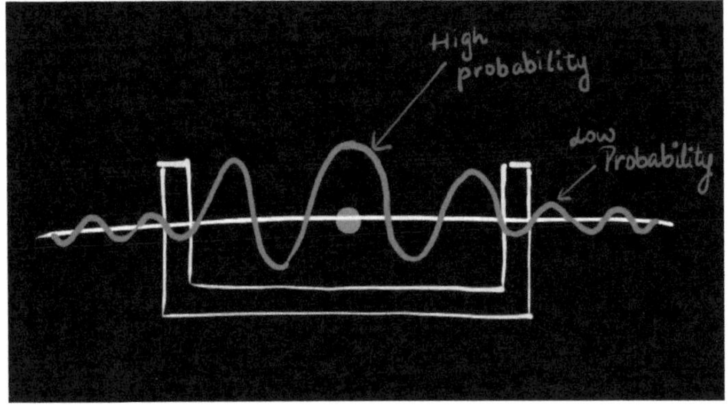

Fig. 7.1: Quantum Tunneling. The quantum object has a small probability to be found on the other side of a finite wall.

The probability of quantum tunnelling is affected by physical quantities like the thickness of the barrier and the mass of the object. It has been experimentally tested that the probability of a human to tunnel through a wall comes out to be 10^{-40}which is very less for tunnelling to occur.

Since all walls are finite, there is always a small probability of an object to tunnel. This also implies that if the wall is thin enough, the wavefunction would allow the particle to be on the other side of the wall place. Therefore, there is a chance that an electron is found on the other side of a barrier upon measurement[9].

7.1: IMPORTANCE OF QUANTUM TUNNELLING

The presence of life on earth is largely dependent on Quantum Tunnelling. All the nuclear fusion energy released by the sun and other stars is a result of quantum tunnelling. We know that protons repel each other due to like-charges and that only a large quantity of heat energy can break the electrostatic forces of repulsion between two protons and combine them together. However, the sun isn't hot enough to be able to overcome the force of repulsion. So, the only method for the combination of protons inside the sun is by tunnelling into each other. This results in the combination of two hydrogen molecules into a helium molecule, releasing large amounts of energy.

The most remarkable effect of quantum tunnelling is the possibility that the universe itself may have come into existence because of it. The most accepted theory of the beginning is that the universe came from an extremely small point called the **Singularity** which contained all the energy of the universe.

During the Big Bang, Singularity expanded exponentially due to an inflationary process that overcame all attractive forces such as gravity. But the big mystery is how did this process eventually begin? This is not well understood but according to the calculations made by the physicist Sir Alexander Vilenkin, the probability that the universe can overcome the energy barrier needed for The Big Bang to occur is not zero, even at the limit when the universe is zero, i.e., absence of space and time. In other words, this means that The Big Bang could occur from nothing. If this calculation is true, quantum tunnelling will surely turn out to be one of the most important natural processes in the universe[10].

CHAPTER EIGHT

The Heisenberg Uncertainty Principle

Heisenberg Uncertainty Principle is a fundamental principle of the universe and arguably the most important one in Quantum Mechanics. This principle primarily explains the behavior of particles and the measurement of the wave function.

The Heisenberg Uncertainty principle explains that you can never simultaneously measure the position and momentum of an object (Fig. 8.1). You can only have probabilistic knowledge about both the position and momentum of a particle. As we know, **p** = **mv**, thus, if we know the location of the particle in space with absolute certainty, we shall have no idea about the velocity of the particle in space. Moreover, this is the principle that governs the wave-particle duality.

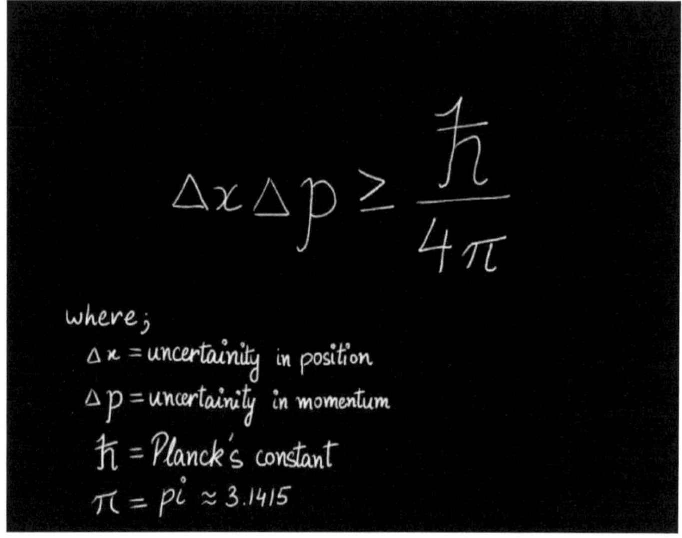

Fig. 8.1: The equation of Heisenberg Uncertainty Principle, defining both position and momentum uncertain for any quantum object.

Uncertainty is explained in terms of measurement. The act of measurement of the position of particles changes the velocity with which the particle travels through space.

We have already studied that everything in the universe behaves both as a particle and a wave at the same time, i.e., wave-particle duality. Quantum Mechanics states that there is no meaning of the exact position or momentum of an object[11].

8.1: PARTICLES VS WAVES

A particle, by definition, exists in a single place at any given point in time. Therefore, we know exactly what the position of the particle is, and it can easily be represented on a graph with a spike of 100% probability at a particular position, and 0% everywhere else.

But waves are much different. They are disturbances across space, without any specific position. Waves possess various properties which can easily be measured, most importantly wavelength, which is the distance between two neighboring crests or two neighboring troughs. However, we can't assign a single position to a wave, it has a high probability of being at lots of different places at the same time.

The wavelength affects the momentum of an object. It is evident that a fast-moving body, like a bullet fired from a gun, has lots of momentum because of its very high speed, which corresponds to a very short wavelength. A heavy object, like an elephant, has high momentum although its velocity is low, which equally corresponds to a short wavelength.

This is the reason why the wave nature of everyday objects is not noticeable. For example, the wavelength of a tennis ball, when thrown in the air has a wavelength of less than 10^{-35} m. We know that such a small value is too tiny to ever be detected. This is because, the smallest measurable length is known as the Planck's Length, equal to $1.6 * 10^{-35}$.

In the case of waves of smaller objects like electrons, we can easily calculate its wavelength, and therefore its momentum. But we don't know the position of the wave with any certainty. On the other hand, we know the position of a particle, but as a particle doesn't have a wavelength, we don't know its momentum.

8.2: QUANTUM OBJECTS

To have a better idea about position and momentum, we must graph a wave that exists in a very small area. For doing this, what we must do is combine waves with different wavelengths. We know the basic principle of the combination of two waves, whenever a peak (or trough) meets another peak (or trough), a larger peak (or trough) is formed. Whenever a peak meets a trough, the wave nullifies and the probability of the particle being there is negligible. This process can be repeated several times to localize the location of the wave to a small region (Fig. 8.2). What we get as a result is what we call a quantum object.

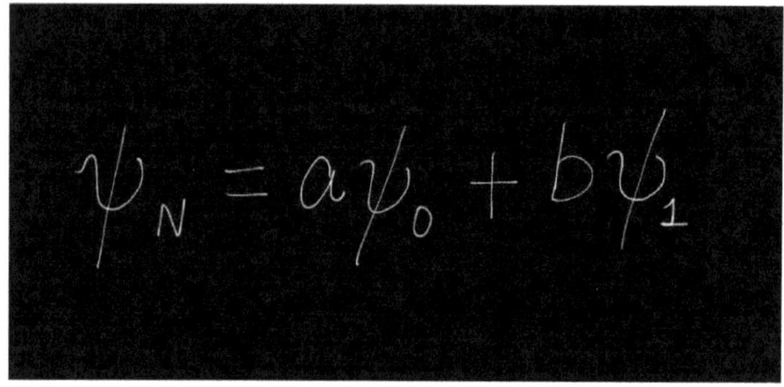

Fig. 8.2: The equation to calculate wave-function of a quantum object formed by adding two waves.

However, in doing so we lost some certainty of both the momentum and position. Although the wavelength has been localized, it can still exist anywhere in that region, so its position is uncertain. Moreover, to localize the wave, we combined different wavelengths, and therefore, we lost certainty about the wavelength of the quantum object, and so its momentum can be the momentum of any of the combined waves, and therefore we lose the certainty of its momentum.

To increase the certainty of its position, more waves are required to be added together, and similarly, if a wave has a certain momentum, the uncertainty of its position increases.

The equation of the Heisenberg Uncertainty Principle also indicates that the momentum of a quantum object can never be zero. This is the reason why particles have Intrinsic Angular Momentum. Moreover, this principle also says that neither position nor momentum can be 100% certain, there is always some uncertainty.

This was all about the Heisenberg Uncertainty Principle, stated first by Werner Heisenberg in 1927. This uncertainty is certainly not due to lack of availability of knowledge, instead is due to the fundamental nature of Quantum Mechanics, wave-particle duality[12].

CHAPTER NINE

SUPER-CONDUCTIVITY

9.1: INTRODUCTION

Quantum Mechanics explains how almost all physics phenomena works are the smallest possible scale. It also includes a strange property exhibited by some materials at extremely low temperatures, Superconductivity.

Superconductivity, on a classical level, refers to the property of certain materials to conduct electricity indefinitely, i.e., without any resistance. When current is flowing through a superconductor, it flows with no resistance and continues to flow through it if the material is in a closed-loop even without any supply of electricity.

9.2: SUPERCONDUCTIVITY OF MATERIALS AND QUANTUM MECHANICS

Heike Onnes, a Dutch physicist, at the beginning of the 20th century, cooled Mercury down to -269°C and ran electricity through it. To his amusement, he found out that the wire had no resistivity, which meant no energy loss even when electricity flows through the metal[13]. He called this state of matter a Superconductor.

To experience superconductivity, it is not necessary to cool the material down to -269°C like in mercury. It has been found that many other materials show superconductivity at much higher temperatures, though all of them are usually less than -123°C (150K).

Observing this phenomenon is extremely unlikely because generally, there is always some loss of energy. This is because, when electrons flow through a conductor, they bump into oppositely charged nuclei of atoms which results in loss of some energy. But in a superconductor, the electrons flow through the conductor without any loss of energy as if there were no atoms in their path. Moreover, when electricity is supplied to a superconductor in a closed-loop, the current will continue to flow through it indefinitely even without any energy source.

9.2.1: Levitation

Superconductors also show the property of levitation. They can levitate a magnet when placed over it. This is because a superconductor expels magnetic flux fields, and therefore doesn't allow the magnetic fields of the magnet to pass through them which other objects normally do at regular temperatures. This is the cause of the levitation of a magnet when placed over a superconducting material.

It seems magical to imagine an object which conducts current perfectly without any loss of energy, but the only way to intuitively understand this phenomenon is through Quantum Mechanics.

9.2.2: Causes of Resistance

On the quantum scale, it is imperative to understand the cause of resistance in the first place to understand superconductivity.

When electric current flows through a conductor, the electrons flow through the material. This flow of electrons isn't perfect though. The electrons continuously bang into the surrounding atoms which results in the loss of some electrical energy. Since the atoms absorb energy, they start to vibrate vigorously at their positions which results in even more collisions between electrons and atoms, and stronger resistance. This is the reason why the flow of electricity increases the temperature of the material.

9.2.3: Formation of Cooper Pair

Now, it's time to recall the Standard Model. The distinction which separates a Fermion and Boson is Pauli Exclusion Principle. This means that any number of Bosons can occupy the same energy level in a quantum system, it is not the case with Fermions. Not more than two Fermions of the same type can occupy the same energy level. This phenomenon of particle physics is extremely useful in our day-to-day life. It is due to the Pauli Exclusion Principle that a solid object doesn't simply pass through another solid object, through the floor, or through the wall.

But this property is not exhibited by Bosons. Instead, Bosons seem to like bunching together, especially at low temperatures. When an electron passes through the lattice of the conductor, it attracts the nearby positively charged ions of the lattice towards it. This creates an area of higher positive charge density. Since that region now has a higher positive charge, other electrons are attracted towards that region. This attraction results in overcoming the repulsive force between a pair of two electrons and causes them to join to form a **Cooper pair** (Fig. 9.1).

Superconductivity

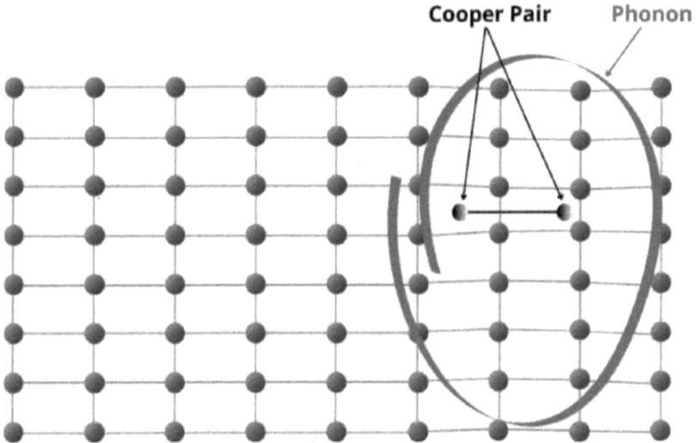

Fig. 9.1: Diagrammatical representation of the lattice of a superconductor. Phonon refers to the positive lattice while the Cooper pair refers to the pair of electrons.

The surrounding lattice made of positive ions shows a collective motion when a Cooper pair passes through it. This part of the lattice is called **Phonon**[14]. Phonons are not only important for understanding superconductivity but are also responsible for the conduction of heat and sound in solids.

The cooper pair remains together until the temperature is high enough to break their bond. So, if the temperatures are low, the Cooper pair remains together and can, thus, be considered as a single particle. Electrons are Spin- ½ particles, so, two of them together behave like Spin-1 particles or Bosons. They now are no longer subject to Pauli Exclusion Principle. Since infinitely many Bosons can fit into an energy level, all the Cooper pairs in a region start acting like a single entity in the lowest energy level, and this state is called Bose-Einstein Condensate. But since these bosons are made of electrons, they have an overall negative charge and can conduct electricity.

When an electron normally moves through the lattice of the conductor, it loses specific quanta of energy. But since the new state is in the lowest energy state, it cannot lose energy anymore. This results in no resistance, or infinite conductivity of the material. This material, hence, becomes a superconductor. Therefore, the main cause of superconductivity is the formation of Cooper pair and its interaction with the Phonon.

9.3: IMPORTANCE OF SUPERCONDUCTIVITY

Superconductivity has various important applications in the current world scenario. The most important is that in Maglev trains, which use superconductivity to function at extremely fast speeds.

Superconductivity is a basic phenomenon, but its functioning is described by Quantum Mechanics. Quantum Mechanics, therefore, successfully describes the true nature of superconducting materials at the quantum scale.

CHAPTER TEN

QUANTUM COMPUTERS

Quantum Computing is by far the most important application of Quantum Mechanics in the real world. Quantum Computers show the potential to revolutionize modern technology with their incredible speed. Quantum Computers can potentially revolutionize medicine, communication, encryption, and artificial intelligence.

However, it must be understood that quantum computers aren't the next generation of supercomputers, they are something else entirely. They are governed by the laws of Quantum Mechanics. Before we can begin to look at their possible applications, we need to understand the fundamental physics that drives the concept of quantum computing.

10.1: ORIGIN OF QUANTUM COMPUTING

Quantum Computing was an idea conceived in the late 20th century. Richard Feynman had encountered a major issue while dealing with quantum objects. Since it was impossible for him to directly observe quantum events, he wanted to design a simulation for the same using his computer. But he quickly understood that it was not possible for his computer to compute so many different scenarios since its computing power was much lesser. Moreover, whenever he added a particle to his simulations, the cost of computations increased exponentially.

Thus, Feynman concluded that classical computers cannot scale fast enough to keep pace with the growing complexity of quantum calculations.

This led him to this magnificent idea of Quantum Computers. Quantum Computers, run by quantum objects and governed by the laws of Quantum Mechanics, are the perfect means to explore the mysteries of the quantum realm[15].

As a result, Feynman started to build a bridge between Quantum Mechanics and Computer science.

10.2: CLASSICAL COMPUTERS VS QUANTUM COMPUTERS

To understand the difference between an ordinary classical computer and a quantum computer, we first need to understand the basics of a classical computer.

A classical computer firstly needs a device for data storage like a hard drive or SSDs (Solid-State Drives). The data transfer occurs between the processors and data storage devices. To fasten this data transfer, the classical computers have RAM (Random Access Memory). But the downside of RAM is that it is very expensive per gigabyte and is highly volatile, which means that the data and RAM can get lost in case of a power cut.

Besides these, each computer has a CPU, which is also regarded as the brain of the computer and is responsible for doing all the computations. All the components of the computer are interconnected using a Motherboard.

The CPU of a classical computer is made from transistors. The transistors can have only two possible values, i.e., binary. It can either be 1 (or true) or 0 (or false). A transistor represents only a binary bit. Sets of such binary numbers represent numbers, letters, or symbols.

10.3: THE IDEA OF QUBITS

The Quantum Computer, governed by the laws of Quantum Mechanics, does not run on classical binary bits. Instead, they use **Qubits**. Qubit is a bit in a superposition of both 1 and 0. Therefore, before measurement, the Qubit is in some combination of both 1 and 0, which in turn means that the Qubits can have infinitely many possible values as compared to a binary bit.

One thing that must be taken care of during the usage of Qubits is that no measurement of any kind is to be done throughout the computation, because measurement will collapse the superposition of Qubits. Both the input and the output resultantly should be in superposition.

Since the Qubits are in a superposition, they follow multiple computational paths at the same time. A Qubit does all the possible computations simultaneously and outputs a classical result, a one or zero. The Qubit is measured at the end of every computation, as a result, the superposition of the Qubits collapses into our final answer.

10.4: QUANTUM ALGORITHMS

One might wonder how is it possible to get the correct output upon measurement since outputs of Qubits are probabilistic. This is where Quantum algorithms come into the picture.

Quantum Algorithms are some extremely clever programs built by scientists using matrices that help in getting maximum accuracy on different computations. This is done by destructive interference on wrong results and constructive interference on correct results.

10.4.1: Complex Numbers

The mathematics of quantum mechanics deals with complex numbers. In quantum computing, it is essential to understand how to plot a complex number on a graph while working on Quantum Algorithms. There are two important terms to know while representing a complex number on a graph: **magnitude** and **phase**. Magnitude is the numerical value of the complex number on the graph, while Phase is the angle between the line joining the number to the origin, and the positive x-axis.

There are several arithmetic operations on complex numbers, and the important ones include:

1. Addition: When two complex numbers of the same phase are added, they output a number with a larger magnitude in the same phase. But when two complex numbers of different phases are added, they output a number with a smaller magnitude.
2. Multiplication: In the multiplication of complex numbers, the second number scales the magnitude of the first, and rotates the phase of the number in its own direction.

While dealing with the mathematics of Quantum Algorithms, the probabilities are written in the form of matrices for easy representation.

10.4.2: State Vectors of Qubits

Qubits are special quantum objects which are in the Superposition of 1 and 0 inside a quantum system. They have a probability distribution which indicates the likeliness of a Qubit to be 0 or 1. The probability distribution of Qubits is calculated from the quantum amplitudes of the qubits. These quantum amplitudes are complex numbers. The collection of the quantum of both possible states of a Qubit is called the state vector of the Qubit.

The probability distribution of different states is obtained by applying the 'Born Rule' to the state vectors of the Qubits. If the probability of Qubit being 0 is SV_1, and that of being 1 is SV_2, then mathematically,

$$(SV_1)^2 + (SV_2)^2 = 1$$

10.4.3: Quantum Single Logic-Gates

For a comprehensive understanding of Quantum Algorithms, we must look at some basic **Quantum Logic-Gates**[16]. Quantum logic-gates are mathematical operations that help to alter the state vectors of Qubits to obtain the desired result. These logic-gates can easily be described using matrices of complex numbers. Single logic gates work only on one qubit at a time.

There are various Quantum logic-gates in practice. There is an Identity Gate (I-Gate) that outputs a Qubit with the same State Vectors. Then there is a Not Gate (X-Gate) which switches the State Vectors of zero and 1. There is also a Z-Gate. It is a very special gate since it rotates the phase of the 1's state vector by pi-radians (180 degrees) without changing the zero's state vector.

Another special but tricky gate is a Hadamard-Gate(H). When a Qubit with equal probabilities of 0 and 1 state is passed through a Hadamard-Gate, the resultant Qubit has a 100% chance of being in the zero-state. When a Qubit with a 100% probability of being in Zero state is passed through this gate, a Qubit with equal probabilities of zero and 1 state is obtained, i.e., the process is reversed. In case a Qubit with a 100% chance of being in 1's state is passed through it, the resultant Qubit has an equal magnitude state vector for both the states, but the phase of 1's state is reversed by pi-radians.

These were a few Quantum logic gates that work on only one Qubit. However, for a quantum computer to work, there are many qubits related to each other through entanglement. As a result of entanglement, the qubits can reach the Bell's state, a state in which either all qubits are zero or all are 1.

10.4.4: Permutations

There are many logic-gates that work on multiple qubits. A certain subset of logic-gates that are common and easy to understand is called Permutations. The Identity-Gate and Not-Gate are also a part of permutations.

Another tricky Permutation is of Controlled-Not Gate. This is used for 2 qubits. This special permutation reverses the State vectors of only the conditions where the first Qubit is 1 without changing the state vectors of the states where the first Qubit is zero (Fig. 10.1).

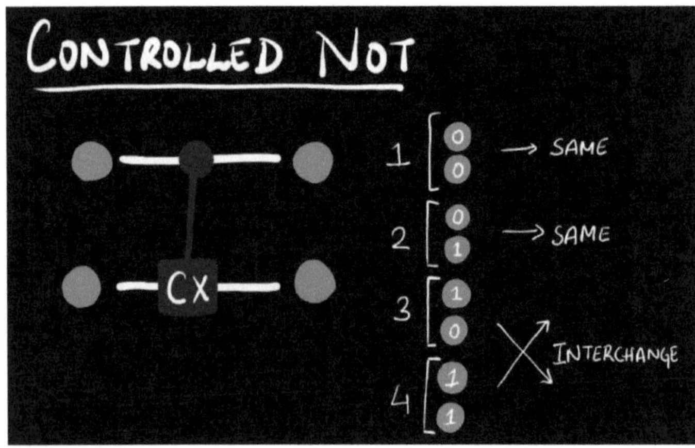

Fig. 10.1: Diagrammatical representation of Controlled-Not Quantum Logic Gate with two Qubits.

The extended version of the Controlled-Not gate is Toffoli Gate, which works on three qubits. This permutation reverses the State vectors of only those conditions where both the first and second Qubits are 1 without changing the state vectors of other states.

Although all the Qubits in a Quantum system are entangled, we can still pass a single Qubit through a Quantum logic-gate because Qubits are physical objects. If we pass only one Qubit through the Hadamard gate in a quantum system of 2 Qubits, we can perform four calculations at a time. Similarly, if we have a quantum system of only 50 Qubits, we can perform over 2^{50} calculations simultaneously.

Using permutations, we can recreate various classical circuits, just like the And-Gate. When two qubits pass through an And-Gate, the output will be 1 only if both are one, otherwise, it would be zero. For this, we take two Input Qubits and one output Qubit. Output qubit is set to zero, so the only possible states are 0-0-0, 1-0-0, 0-1-0, and 1-1-0. When this state is passed through the Toffoli-Gate, 0-0-0, 1-0-0, and 0-1-0 have the same output, but 1-1-0 changes to 1-1-1. And this represents the And-Gate (Fig. 10.2). In this way, circuits used in classical mechanics can also be used in Quantum systems.

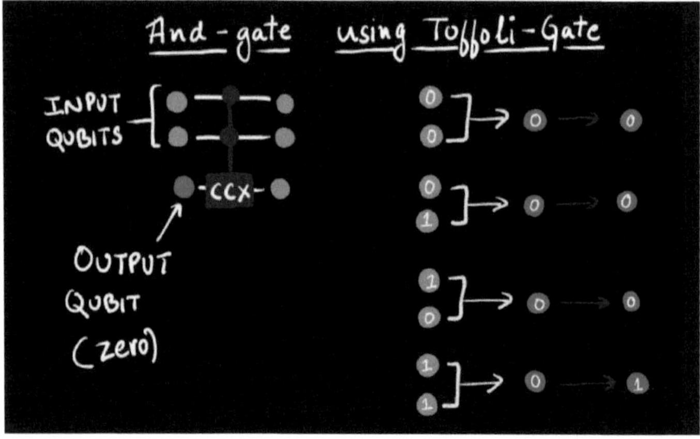

Fig. 10.2: Diagrammatical representation of And-Gate from classical mechanics, built-in Quantum Computers using Toffoli Quantum Logic-Gate with three Qubits.

A huge benefit of Quantum logic gates is that the inputs can easily be restored by reversing the Logic-gate. This phenomenon is true for all logic gates and circuits designed from it.

10.4.5: Grover's Algorithm

Grover was an Indo-American scientist who worked closely on quantum computing. He designed the "Amplitude Amplification" algorithm, popularly known as Grover's Algorithm. This algorithm increases the chances for the output to be in the state we are interested in, just like finding factors of a particular number by random multiplication of numbers.

Grover's Algorithm has two parts, the first consisting of the states that we are interested in amplifying. This is called the "Oracle". It takes in all the possible state vectors of different states and rotates the phase of only the required state by 180 degrees. This is done by passing the output of all states through the Z-Gate. Whenever the output is one, the Z-gate rotates the phase by 180 degrees, and whenever it is zero, it remains unaffected.

In the second part, Hadamard-Gate is applied to all the states repeatedly after flipping the phases by 180 degrees each time. This results in an increase in the efficiency of the quantum system. When we apply Grover's algorithm repeatedly, we end up with only the interested states.

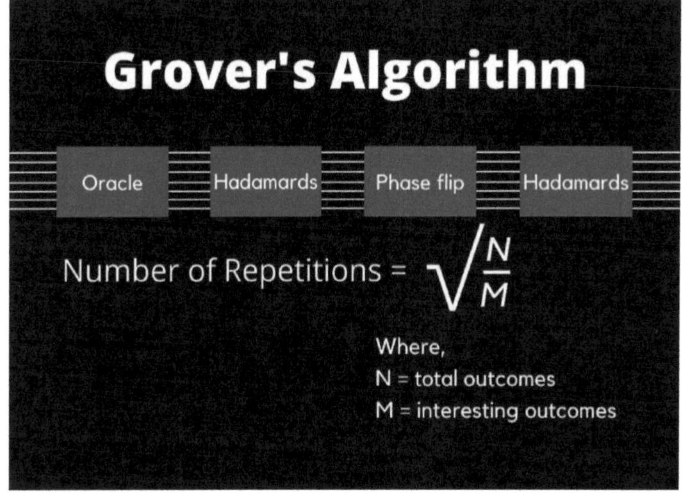

Fig. 10.3: Diagrammatical representation of Grover's Algorithm. The figure describes the effectiveness of Quantum systems over classical systems.

Fig. 10.3 shows the power of Quantum Computing since the number of computations required is much less than in classical computing where it is equal to *N*.

10.5: POWER OF QUANTUM COMPUTER

Quantum computers don't do regular tasks faster than normal classical computers. Instead, they do more tasks at a time. For example, if a classical computer is to solve a difficult maze, it will take time in finding the correct path by going through all the paths one by one. A quantum computer on the other hand can go through all the possible paths at the same time and provide you with the correct path of the maze almost instantaneously[17].

The number of states a quantum system can explore at once can be derived from the formula 2^n where n = *number of Qubits* in the system. For example, a quantum system with 300 Qubits can go through more states at an instant than there are particles in the entire universe. This is the power of quantum computers. However, making and storing a quantum computer isn't an easy task either. It is hard to build because it is completely isolated from the rest of the world.

The Qubits are in a superposition, so they must never be measured, because of which, they must always be isolated. Moreover, the temperature of Qubits must always be very low, as low as 0.015 K, just above absolute zero. This is because heat fluctuations in the environment can alter or destroy the superposition of Qubits by interacting with them. The circuit of the Qubits is also very finely designed to provide for quick and easy interactions between Qubits.

10.6: USES OF QUANTUM COMPUTERS

The main use of Quantum computing is in generating **Quantum Simulations**. Even the current generation supercomputers are unable to simulate the quantum processes fast enough. Quantum Computers, running on Quantum mechanics, can perform these simulations at an exponentially faster rate.

Another use of Quantum computers is in breaching **cyber security**. The entire online data is protected using cryptography, using algorithms such as RSA and Hash. These techniques are so hard to breach that a classical computer would take ages to break. But a quantum computer can make these cryptography methods useless with its super-fast calculations. If you want to find an extremely difficult password using a supercomputer, it might take the supercomputer around 200 years to do so, but a quantum computer with the same number of Qubits can find it in less than 10 seconds.

A quantum computer can also revolutionize **medicine**. The simulations done using a classical computer aren't as efficient as required to study the effects of medicinal drugs on our bodies. Using a quantum computer, these simulations can easily be conducted to test drugs before using them on an individual. By adding machine learning algorithms to it, it is possible for a quantum computer to study the effects of different proteins on our bodies and develop a cure for the same by itself, thereby reducing a significant number of tasks of healthcare researchers.

These are a few of the many ways that Quantum Computers can revolutionize the world in the times to come. The quantum world, howsoever strange it may seem, has many underlying benefits which are still waiting to be put into practice, and Quantum computing is surely one of them.

CHAPTER ELEVEN

QUANTUM FIELD THEORY

Quantum Field Theory is another astounding theory of Quantum Mechanics. It deals with the ways in which different quantum particles interact. It bridges two extremely successful theories together, Quantum Mechanics and Special Relativity.

11.1: LOOPHOLES IN QUANTUM MECHANICS

We know that Quantum Mechanics deals with the behavior of quantum objects, their evolution through time, the distribution of the location of particles, and many more such phenomena. Howsoever perfect it may seem; it has two major loopholes.

Quantum Mechanics doesn't describe the situation when the number of particles varies over time. However, this is extremely common in a real-world scenario. We commonly see an electron absorb a photon, or a photon splitting into an electron-positron pair.

The second major loophole of quantum mechanics is that it describes all particles independently. There is no relation between two particles of the same type in Quantum Mechanics. But all electrons, for example, have the same properties, like mass and charge.

11.2: QUANTUM FIELDS

Special Relativity describes the universe as a fabric of spacetime. When we fill the universe with matter, we consequently realize that all particles of the same family type are completely identical. Since all of them are identical, we can consider that all such particles are local manifestations of the same underlying object, a field.

In mathematics, a field is a fluid that occupies the entire space of the universe, and every point in it is filled with mathematical objects. The mathematical objects can either be numbers, vectors, or complex objects like spinors[18].

However, the mathematical objects have some restrictions imposed on them by Special Relativity. It imposes that the objects must respect the symmetries of translation, rotation, and changing the frame of reference.

These symmetries are respected only by certain objects, and the parameter that determines it is none other than particle spin. If the object is a number, it is said to be a Spin-0 particle since it doesn't vary with the rotation of space around it. A vector is said to be a Spin-1 particle since it represents a direction, and therefore its appearance depends on its orientation. They have Spin-1 because a vector describes a full turn when the space around it is rotated by a full turn. The Quantum spin of a particle in this scenario depends on the number of times it rotates by a full turn when rotated by 360°. In the same way, spinors have spin ½ because they rotate one full turn after two full rotations of the space around them.

These fields must obey special relativity, and to do that, they must respect the conservation of energy, momentum, angular momentum, and velocity of the center of mass. In case we have a field of complex numbers, another essential fundamental property is also conserved by the field, the electric charge.

Since the field is made up of quantum objects, the field also behaves based on quantum principles. The quantum fields are in a superposition, and since they describe the evolution of particles over time, the evolution is in the state of superposition too. A quantum object evolves in all possible ways inside a quantum field simultaneously with different probabilities.

As we move from a classical field to a quantum field, a very interesting property is observed. Just like electrons have different energy levels inside an atom, the quantum fields also have different energy levels, which means that they can only contain an integer number of disturbances, fixed quanta of energy, which can appear or disappear as integers. This quantum of energy represents a particle. Inside quantum fields, particles propagate like disturbances that can appear or disappear.

The quantum fields also have another interesting property. They contain fluctuations, which keep on moving in and out of existence. These fluctuations are called virtual particles. They are virtual, i.e., they cannot be observed. The reason for the same is that they exist in very small numbers, so small that it is strictly impossible for us to measure.

11.3: QUANTUM FIELD THEORY AND THE STANDARD MODEL

There are three basic types of fields, fields with Spin-0 particles, fields with Spin- ½ particles, and fields with Spin-1 particles. Each spin is associated with a different family of particles present in the Standard Model.

The Bosons, i.e., Photons, Gluons, Z-Bosons, and W-Bosons are all Spin-1 particles and have vector representation in quantum fields.

The Fermions, i.e., Quarks, Electrons, and Neutrinos are all Spin- ½ particles and have are represented by spinors inside quantum fields.

The Higgs Bosons are Spin-0 particles, and their fields are represented by Complex Numbers. Although it is strictly impossible for a particle to have Spin-0, the Higgs particle is an exception (Fig. 11.1).

Fig. 11.1: Representation of various particles of the Standard Model along with their electric charge and quantum-spin.

Generally, all quantum fields have internal symmetries which help us distinguish between particles. Since the charge of particles is conserved over time, we have the second variants of all charged particles, and these are called Anti-Particles. They have the opposite charge and can be considered as the complex conjugates of regular particles. Similarly, Quarks field has another symmetry, color symmetry.

11.4: QUANTUM INTERACTIONS

Our model of Quantum Field is almost complete. But there is one problem. All the symmetries of the universe result in the infinite motion of particles in a straight line path without any interactions. For the model universe to be complete, it is imperative to add the last fundamental property to it, the interaction between fields.

The most fundamental interaction in quantum mechanics is the emission or absorption of a photon by an electron. This phenomenon has been explained in detail in the next chapter, Quantum Electrodynamics. It describes the evolution of electrons over time and how they interact by mutual exchange of electrons. The interaction of electrons is due to the loss of photons which also takes away a part of its momentum. The evolution of particles is in a state of superposition, it evolves through all possible scenarios at the same time, with definite probability[19]. To each evolution, there is a complex equation that helps in determining the overall interaction from all possible scenarios.

11.5: SUMMARY

This was the basic idea about Quantum Field Theory. Quantum Field Theory, in general, is the mathematical description of the universe that satisfies the symmetries of special relativity. It thereby describes a universe that can co-exist with the constraints of special relativity and provides a better description of the model universe where particles can interact, be lost, or gained.

Quantum Field Theory is probably the best available description of the universe backed by experiments and mathematical uniformity. However, there is a problem. Quantum field theory fails to work along with general relativity. These two theories simply can't co-exist. Therefore, is a need to modify either of the theories or to come up with a new theory, which can describe the universe completely, without any setbacks. There are theories that describe Quantum Mechanics with General Relativity, like Quantum loop gravity and String Theory, but they haven't been experimentally verified yet. Thus, Quantum Field Theory is the best theory to date describing an accurate model of the universe. It is one of the most successful theories in history, providing mathematical results with astounding accuracy, more than any other theory of physics.

CHAPTER TWELVE

QUANTUM ELECTRODYNAMICS

12.1: INTRODUCTION TO QUANTUM ELECTRODYNAMICS

We are aware of the general idea that two electrons repel when close to each other. This property of electrons is very useful to explain the everyday activities of our daily life. Excluding Gravity and Radioactivity, almost all universal phenomena are a result of the activities of electrons.

On the classical level, we might describe the repulsion of electrons due to electromagnetic force. But what we must keep in mind is Electromagnetism is a theory of classical physics but Electrons, on the other hand, are quantum objects governed by laws of Quantum Mechanics. Therefore, it is necessary to reconcile electromagnetism with Quantum Mechanics. This is where Quantum Electrodynamics comes into the picture. Quantum Electrodynamics explains the interaction between electrons on the quantum scale. Quantum Electrodynamics in essence is a category of Quantum Field Theory, which describes the electric field of electron-type particles, and the electromagnetic field of Photons.

Quantum Electrodynamics is the most precise model ever created in the history of Physics with a precision of about ±0.0000001. It is truly an elegant model which uses simple diagrams called Feynman Diagrams to calculate one of the most fundamental phenomena of Physics, electromagnetic repulsions of electrons.

12.2: ELECTRIC VS ELECTROMAGNETIC FIELD

Quantum Electrodynamics is a sub-classification of Quantum Field Theory. It indicates that Spacetime is comprised of two fluids made of mathematical objects. One is the electric field, and another is the electromagnetic field. These fields contain packets of energy which are called particles. Electrons in quantum electrodynamics are disturbances that propagate like waves inside the electric field. Electromagnetic field, on the other hand, contains specific quanta of energy called photons which can appear or disappear[20].

The electric field is different from the electromagnetic field because they are made of different mathematical objects. Electric fields have spinors. Mathematically, electrons are complex numbers. As they move through time, their phase rotates. This is called the electric charge of the electron. As an analogy, consider that the phase of an electron rotates clockwise, and therefore it has a unit negative charge. There is another set of particles that rotate anti-clockwise. These particles can also be imagined as an e^{-1} particle going back in time. This is called anti-electron (positron).

Photons on the other hand are real numbers. They only have a particular magnitude but no phase. This is the reason why photons do not possess electric charge.

12.3: FEYNMAN DIAGRAMS

To understand the behavior of electrons when brought near each other, we use two particles and represent them using lines. The line which extends towards the future is of an electron, and the line that extends towards the past is called a positron. In Feynman diagrams, photons are represented by a sine wave. The two fields, i.e., the electric and the electromagnetic field, react with each other at Interaction Vertices which describes the real-world evolution of particles (Fig. 12.1).

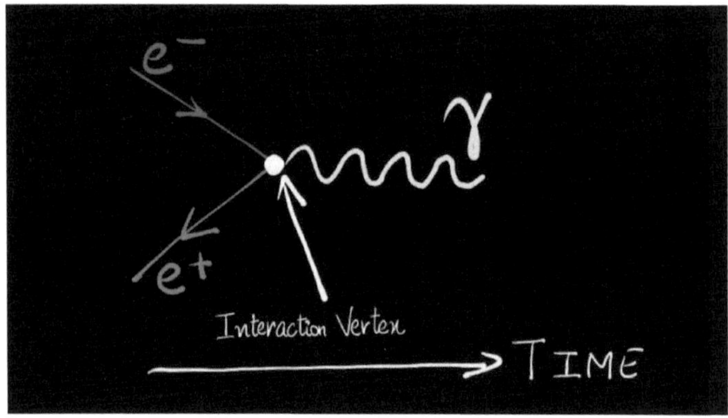

Fig. 10.1: Diagrammatical representation of Controlled-Not Quantum Logic Gate with two Qubits.

Interaction vertices require a photon particle and two electron-type particles. The electron-type particles can be either two electrons or positrons depending upon their orientation with time.

Common interactions include an electron-emitting or absorbing a photon with a slight change in its momentum. The positron could also emit or absorb an electron in the same way. Less common, but the possible reaction could be, an electron combines with a positron to form a photon or even a photon dividing into an electron-positron pair.

Quantum electrodynamics allows all these interactions to occur, provided that the overall momentum on either side of the Interaction Vertex is equal, i.e., the law of conservation of momentum holds true. Also, the overall electric charge must also be conserved, so there is always an arrow pointing towards the vertex and an arrow away from the vertex at the same time.

One of the simplest interactions between two electrons could be one of them emitting a photon, thereby losing a part of its momentum, while the other electron absorbing it (Fig. 12.2). Since photons behave like waves, they can be exchanged in the direction opposite to their momentum and therefore can result in two electrons moving towards each other instead. An electron can also emit and reabsorb one or more photons by itself.

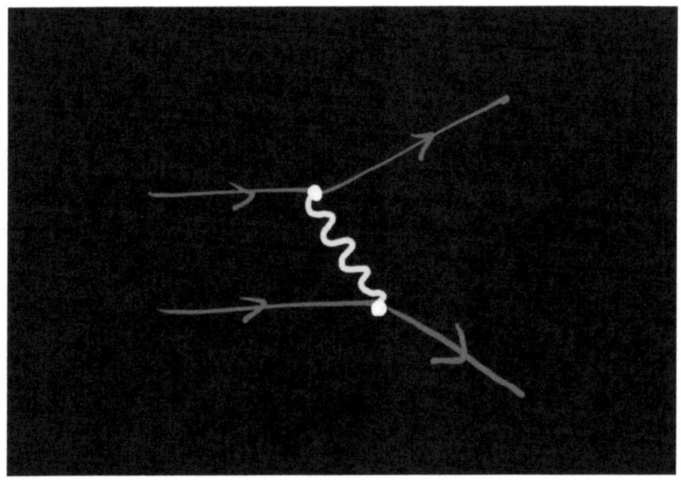

Fig. 10.2: Diagrammatical representation of And-Gate from classical mechanics, built in Quantum Computers using Toffoli Quantum Logic-Gate with three Qubits.

These, however, are simple scenarios. There is, to an extent, no limit to the number of interactions between two electrons at a time. Two electrons might exchange one, two or more electrons, and this exchange can occur at different places or times. They can even give out a photon which converts into an electron-positron pair which might recombine to form a photon (Fig. 12.3).

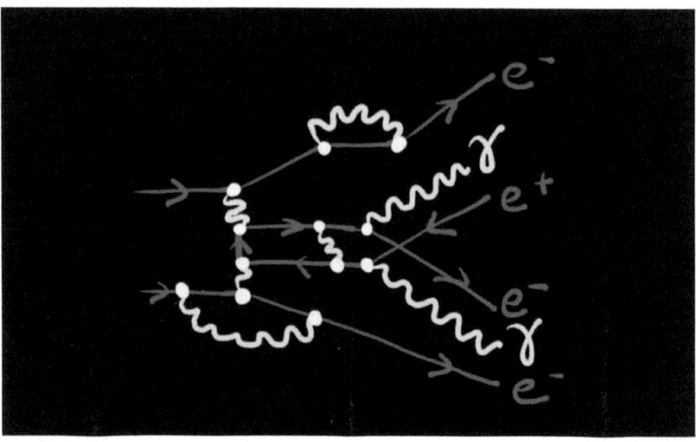

Fig. 10.3: Diagrammatical representation of Grover's Algorithm. The figure describes the effectiveness of Quantum systems over classical systems.

We might by now realize that there is an infinite number of possible interactions between two electrons when placed close by. The number of particles formed at the end of an interaction might not be equal to that before the interaction. If we stop the evolution of the field after a certain time, it is possible to have more particles in our outcome stage than there were in the initial instance. The representation of the evolution of electric and electromagnetic fields is called the Feynman Diagram[21].

In Feynman diagrams, the initial and final stages represent the particles, which can be experimentally detected. The in-between stage, however, cannot be detected can sometimes be extremely strange, and is composed of virtual particles. These intermediaries show us how the electrons interact at a distance. The study of Feynman Diagrams isn't as easy as it seems. Behind each Feynman diagram, there is an extremely difficult mathematical equation formed by combining equations of different parts of the diagram.

One might argue that the virtual particles are undetectable, and therefore easily ignore them. However, these virtual particles (intermediaries) explain the interaction between the electric and the electromagnetic field, and thereby explain one of the most important phenomena in physics, the behavior of electrons.

12.4: PROBABILITY CALCULATIONS

We know that there are infinitely many possible interactions between two electrons, and we are interested in all of them.

We first create a catalog of as many Feynman diagrams as possible. The interactions could be simple or complex, involving one or many interaction vertices. We are interested in all possible scenarios because the electrons are in a state of superposition, so they take up all the possible scenarios at the same time, and what we observe is all a result of probability.

Since each Feynman Diagram is associated with its corresponding equation, it is possible to have a number representing each scenario. This number is called the Amplitude of the respective scenario. The amplitudes of different scenarios might end up being constructive or destructive depending on the sign.

For calculating the overall amplitude, we can neglect the more complex scenarios and focus on the easier ones since it is practically impossible to calculate all the infinitely many scenarios. It has been experimentally verified that such a method also gives out reasonably accurate results.

As things turn out, the maximum probability is to find the electrons with slightly different momenta due to slight movement away from each other. This results in the real-world phenomenon of electronic repulsions.

12.5: ADVANTAGES OF QUANTUM ELECTRODYNAMICS

There are some major advantages of Quantum Electrodynamics. It allows us to describe the behavior of electrons, positrons, and photons with astounding probability. This theory explains, at the fundamental level, all the laws of optics, the behavior of light in different media, and Maxwell's equations which govern the electric and magnetic fields. Most importantly, it explains the interaction between electrons which describes almost all the forces on our scale. This theory, with its elegant diagrams and extremely precise mathematics, has also enabled scientists to understand the behavior of electrons in magnetic fields.

Quantum Electrodynamics is one of the breakthrough theories of physics, which help in calculating accurate results of almost up to 10 significant figures. It is, by any measure, the most successful theory of all time.

CHAPTER THIRTEEN

THE THEORY OF RELATIVITY

13.1: INTRODUCTION

The Theory of Relativity was introduced by Sir Albert Einstein in the early 20th century. The theory of relativity has two parts, General Relativity, describing the mysterious force of Gravity, and Special relativity, dealing mostly with Time Dilation.

The theory of Relativity doesn't deal with the quantum world. However, it is important to understand it because of its differences from Quantum Mechanics. The theory of General Relativity does not work hand in hand with Quantum Mechanics! In fact, these both can't exist together. Thus, it is imperative to understand the theory of Relativity. That said, the other part of the theory, Special Relativity works quite well with Quantum Mechanics, especially in Quantum Field Theory and Quantum Electrodynamics.

13.2: GENERAL RELATIVITY

Discovering General Relativity wasn't an easy task for even the smartest man on the planet. Moreover, initially, nobody agreed to this idea because it proved the concept of

Gravity proposed by Sir Isaac Newton wrong.

It all started with a thought experiment by Einstein while working in his patent office as a clerk. He had a brilliant imagination, imagining what would be the experience of a man while falling from the top of the building. Most of us might think that he would be heavily injured or would die but Einstein saw the scenario differently. He imagined the period while the man was in mid-air, and not when he would have fallen. Einstein realized that the only force acting on the man would be the force of gravity and since the ground is not pushing the man in an upward direction, the man would not feel any weight, just like a man in the middle of space.

Then he considered the two other scenarios simultaneously. In one, a man is weighing himself on a weighing machine inside his room on earth, and the same person measuring his weight in a spacecraft moving with an acceleration of 9.8 m s^{-1}. Einstein realized that the weight of the person in both the scenarios would be the same, and therefore concluded that there was a difference between acceleration and gravity (Fig. 13.1).

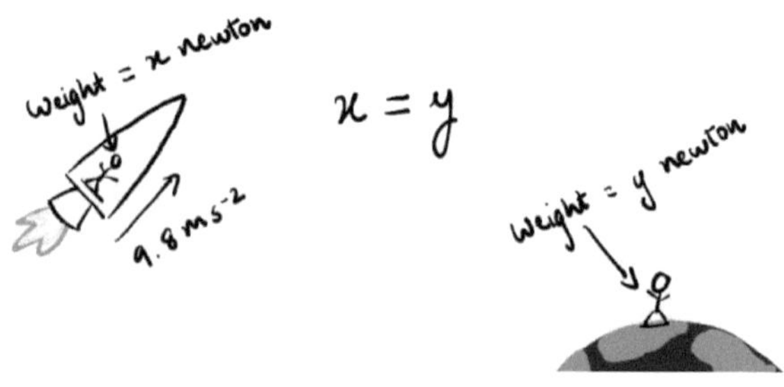

Fig. 13.1: Diagrammatical representation of Sir Albert Einstein's thought experiment. The weight of a man on

earth shall be equal to the weight of the man on a spaceship accelerating at 9.8 m s^{-1}. This proves that gravity is the acceleration produced on a body due to the curvature of spacetime.

Einstein also considered the scenario when the man, standing in the spacecraft moving with an acceleration of 9.8 m s^{-1} uses a torchlight and sees the landing point of the light rays. Since the spacecraft is accelerating upwards, there should be slight bending of light downwards due to the acceleration, howsoever small it may be. He conducted the same experiment in his laboratory and observed the same thing[22].

Einstein concluded that there was something mischievous going on, since we all know that light travels the shortest distance between two points, how is it possible for light to bend on its path since the shortest path between two points is a straight line. Einstein thought of another scenario, when an object moves from one place on earth to another far-off place, the shortest path between the two places is always curved since the surface of the earth is not flat. Einstein concluded from this thought experiment that light must bend when in the influence of a gravitational field.

Einstein concluded from his observations that the shortest path between two places might not be a straight line, instead, there is a curvature of space around mass and energy because of which the light rays must curve to take the shortest path.

Einstein, with the help of his friend Marcel Grossman, figured out the extremely complex mathematics of spacetime. However, during that time, everyone believed in Newtonian Physics that space and time are both fixed, and Gravity is a mysterious force acting at a distance. But according to Einstein, gravity was not a force, but a thing that emerges from the interaction of space and matter.

With the new theory, the orbits of planets could now be explained not on the bases of a force acting at a distance but by using interactions between space and massive objects. The mathematics of the theory of Relativity did wonders. It predicted the mysterious orbit of planet Mercury which not even the equations of Newtonian Gravity could describe.

Even after all the mathematical proofs, many people still disagreed with the idea of spacetime curvature and general relativity. But the full-proof validation of the theory of relativity came during a solar eclipse. The theory predicted the change in the position of stars near the sun during the eclipse due to the bending of light around the curvature of spacetime near the sun. This phenomenon confirmed that the theory of relativity is correct (Fig. 13.2).

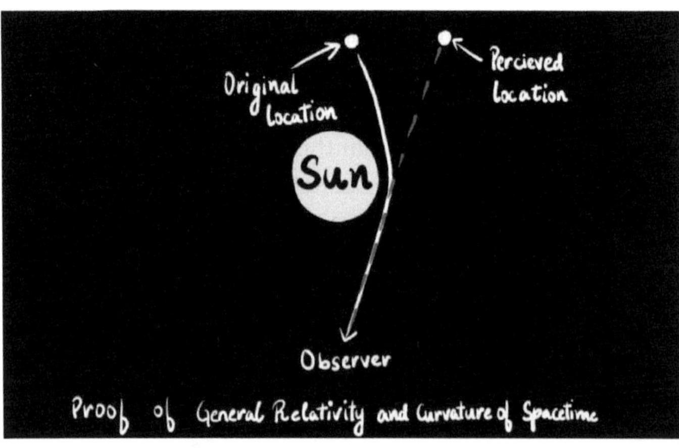

Fig. 13.2: Diagrammatical representation of apparent change in position of a star due to bending of light due to

curvature of spacetime around massive objects.

13.2.1: Relativity as Gravity

Einstein thought the bending of spacetime around massive objects was just like the effect produced by a heavy ball kept on a trampoline. If any smaller ball is kept on the trampoline, it would immediately roll down towards the center of the trampoline, where indeed is the heavier ball.

However, this analogy isn't perfect. Space is three-dimensional, and not two-dimensional like the surface of the trampoline. Still, the analogy works quite well to understand the basic concept behind spacetime. It is imperative to understand that the bending of spacetime is maximum when the curvature is maximum, which is probably the reason for maximum gravity near the equator and minimum near the poles[23].

13.3: SPECIAL RELATIVITY

Till now we only talked about the curvature of space around massive objects, but we did not talk about its influence on 'time'. This phenomenon is explained using the other part of the Theory of Relativity, Special Relativity.The theory of Special Relativity is much more intuitive to understand. It can easily be understood by the following example.

When a rocket is moving in space at a constant velocity with respect to Earth, from the perspective of a man on earth the rocket is in motion, whereas, from the perspective of a man inside the rocket, the Earth is in motion with the same velocity in the opposite direction. This is the basic meaning of relativity. The motion of objects is relative to the observer.

In the same way, if a man inside the rocket throws a ball forward with a certain velocity (V_1), the man observes the ball to move with the speed V_1, but for a man on Earth, the speed of the ball is $V_1 + V_2$ where V_2 is the speed of the rocket. This infers that the speed of an object is also relative to point of observation.

But when the same scenario is used to measure the speed of light, our original inference fails, the speed of light is always 299,792,458 m s^{-1} irrespective of the observers. The speed of light is fundamental to the structure of the universe and does not vary, unlike other scenarios.

Einstein conducted another magnificent thought experiment. He considered himself to stand in front of the train track and see two simultaneous lightning bolts strike on either side of him. For him, the two events were simultaneous, but it would be different for a man on a train moving with the speed of light. Einstein thought that if relativity is correct then the man on the train would observe the lightning closer to him before the farther one. But how could this be possible, how could the scenario not be simultaneous for the man in the train, but simultaneous for the man outside the train.

13.3.1: Time Dilation

Einstein had to choose between two possible scenarios. Either Newton's laws were incomplete, or the speed of light (299,792,458 m s^{-1}) calculated by scientist Sir Maxwell was not a universal constant. Einstein thought that the two notions could co-exist by making a small change in Newton's laws. Since Speed = D/T, since the speed is doubled and distance is constant, the time should be reduced to half, i.e., the time should pass slower such that the speed of light remains a constant (Fig. 13.3).

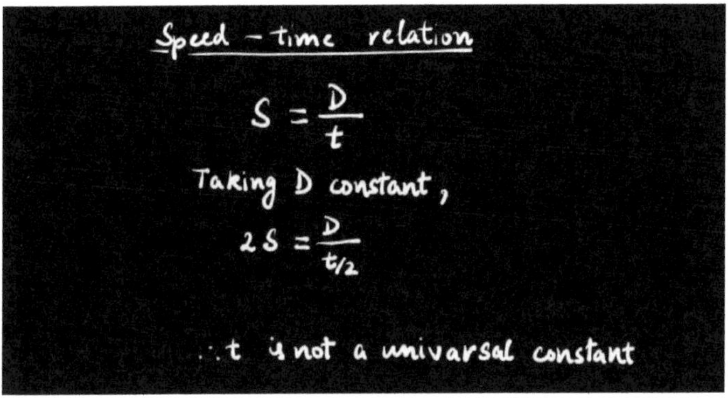

Fig. 13.3: Equational proof that time is not a universal constant, derived from Sir Albert Einstein's thought experiment.

Therefore, according to Special Relativity, time is not a constant. He called this absurdity of time "Time Dilation" (Fig. 13.4). Time dilation affects everything, even our clocks, and watches. The time dilation depends on the velocity of the object with which it travels. Even though generally time dilation while traveling even in airplanes is in nanoseconds, some effect of time dilation is always observed on all clocks. This phenomenon is kept in mind while setting the clocks on geo-navigation and satellites.

Time Dilation

$$\Delta t = \frac{\Delta t_0}{\sqrt{1 - \frac{v^2}{c^2}}}$$

Fig. 13.4: The equation of Time Dilation. Here, v = *velocity of object*, c = *velocity of light*, and t_0 = *one-position time (time perceived at rest).*

Einstein also believed that time should have its own dimension since it is not a constant. Therefore, he called it four-dimensional spacetime, with 3 dimensions of space and one of time. Spacetime is a four-dimensional fabric that runs throughout the universe.

13.3.2: Length Contraction

Another very interesting phenomenon resulting from time dilation is length contraction. When a rocket is moving through space, the back of the rocket would be slightly ahead in time while the front would be slightly back in time[24]. This can easily be done using the following experiment.

A person inside the rocket is asked to stand in the middle of the room and glow two torches at the same time in both directions, forwards and backward. The light moving towards the back of the rocket would reach before reaching the front since the back of the rocket is moving towards the light source and vice versa. However, since the speed of light is always constant, the time would pass faster in the back of the rocket than in the front. Since the back of the rocket is ahead in time, and the front is back in time, the rocket appears to shrink lengthwise and resulting in length contraction.

The contraction of objects on a day-to-day basis is unobservable. For example, an extremely fast car moving on a highway shrinks by less than the size of an atom. However, there is always a length contraction for fast-moving objects. The faster the object moves through space, the greater is the observed length contraction of the object. For example, for an object moving with the speed $2.55 * 10^8$ m s^{-1}, the length of the object reduces to half.

13.4: PROBLEMS WITH GENERAL RELATIVITY ON A QUANTUM SCALE

General relativity is an accurate theory as it correctly predicts spacetime curvature up to 10^{-4} m. However, the theory doesn't work together with Quantum Mechanics. It is yet to be described how Gravity works at the quantum scale, or even at small scales. Just for an example, a hydrogen atom has one proton and one electron. The electron revolves around the proton of the atom. But we know that electrons are in a state of superposition when they are not being measured and therefore, are in all possible positions around the proton until measurement. Since electrons have mass, according to general relativity, they should curve spacetime around themselves. But since electrons are in a superposition, the spacetime should curve around all the possible positions of electrons. General relativity doesn't answer this question.

Another problem is about black holes. General Relativity fails inside a black hole. It yields an infinite spacetime curvature since matter and energy are compressed to an infinitely small point called Singularity. Also, general relativity predicts the loss of all information (except charge, mass, and spin) about the particles when it enters the black hole. However, according to **Quantum Mechanics Information Paradox**, the information can never be lost from a quantum object.

The major problem while trying to experimentally verify Quantum Gravity is the weakness of gravitational force itself. For example, the entire earth or a huge planet or satellite is required to keep the man on the surface. However, these objects are massive, so we can't observe quantum effects using such objects. But when we go to minute scales, like electrons, the force of gravity is so less that it can easily be ignored. For example, two electrons at a separation of 1 cm would attract each other with a force 10^{-24} times the electrostatic repulsions. This value is so small that it has seemingly no effect on electrons.

Moreover, it is believed that Graviton, if it exists, is of a size less than Planck's length, the smallest measurable length. Therefore, it is impossible to measure a graviton according to Quantum Mechanics. The standard model fails to accommodate Graviton as well. Including Graviton in the standard model gives absurd results like infinities or zeros which can't be removed. Therefore, we can't describe gravity on the quantum scale simply using the equations of the Standard Model.

To unite quantum mechanics with general relativity, there have been various theories that have popped up describing the true nature of reality. Some of the most famous ones include the String Theory and the Quantum

Loop Gravity. Although none of there have been experimentally verified, they are extremely promising and maybe, the true theory of the universe.

CHAPTER FOURTEEN

The String Theory

The String Theory is a highly conceptual theory that aims to bridge the gap between Quantum Mechanics and General relativity. The name suggests the true nature of reality itself, strings. The String theory suggests that in the deepest scale of reality, inside the subatomic particles present in the Standard Model, are thin, one-dimensional strings, either closed or open, vibrating differently to produce different particles.

The current notion of particle physics isn't complete in one sense, it fails to describe a fundamental force of nature, Gravity. This is where the String Theory comes into the picture. This theory essentially describes the universe made of tiny inextensible strings, which successfully predict and describe the force of gravity based on principles of relativity.

The basic idea of string theory is that on a quantum scale, objects are not simply point-particles, they are open or closed strings, have tension, and vibrate differently, accounting for the different types of particles present in the universe. Different types of vibration are associated with a different number of ripples during vibration.

This idea of the universe helps us to predict the existence of Graviton, the force particle responsible for the force of gravity on the quantum scale.

14.1: QUANTUM FIELDS AND STRINGS THEORY

We have discussed earlier that there are different fields for different types of particles, but here things get interesting. Inside a quantum field, if particles are dimensionless points, they'll trace a trajectory over time. However, according to String Theory, particles are made of strings, therefore, they trace a surface and not merely a trajectory.

We can consider a quantum system made of dimensionless particles which travel through time and interact with other particles by emitting or absorbing them. These interactions seem instantaneous with point objects. The interactions of strings, on the other hand, are continuous because particles are emitted gradually. Strings can easily duplicate themselves or recombine. Thus, String Theory deals with interactions and there is no need to add them manually, like in Quantum Mechanics. It is due to this property of String Theory that it successfully describes Gravity[25]. Even better, String Theory also describes how a Graviton interacts with other particles, thereby describing Quantum Gravity.

14.2: PROBLEMS WITH THE STRING THEORY

There are three major problems with the model of String Theory we considered till now. Firstly, the strings succeed only in describing Bosons. That's why this version of String Theory is also called 'Bosonic String Theory'. But this theory doesn't include Fermions at all.

The second problem is that this theory predicts the existence of a particle called Tachyon. The problem with

Tachyon is, its predicted mass is an imaginary number, square root of -1. This indicates that the theory isn't completely stable.

The third problem is extra-dimensions. As known to us, there are three dimensions of space and one dimension of time. However, the mathematics of String Theory is such that it required 25-dimensions of space to exist, which is realistically impossible.

14.3: SUPERSTRINGS

To get rid of all the problems with the String Theory, various scientists have pushed the theory a little further. To include Fermions to String Theory, spinors have been added to the Strings, just like those present in Quantum Fields. The result is a solution to two of the three problems stated above. Fermions are now included in the String Theory. Also, the String Theory no longer predicts the Tachyon, the particle which was causing a problem. This more complete description of the String Theory is called Superstring Theory[26, 27].

The Superstring theory also results in the creation of an internal symmetry between Fermions and Bosons. According to the Superstring Theory, the number of types of Fermions should be equal to the number of types of Bosons. This is called **super-symmetry**. Superstring theory also significantly reduces the number of dimensions required for the theory to be true. Earlier, a total of 26 dimensions were required for the theory to be true, but due to supersymmetry, now the theory requires a world of 10 dimensions.

14.3.1: Dimensions of the Universe

Unfortunately, this problem hasn't been resolved. The theory, howsoever promising it may be, doesn't seem to fit into our universe which has only four dimensions. But scientists haven't given up on the idea of additional dimensions. Some believe that our universe is a three-dimensional slice of a larger 9-dimensional super-universe. This idea is called the Brane Bulk Model of the universe.

Another more promising ideology for the same is that the other six invisible dimensions are extremely small and are curled up on themselves because of which they cannot be observed. The idea of additional dimensions might turn out to be true. The addition of extra dimensions describes the presence of a mass on an object. We know that according to Standard Model, all particles are massless, and their interaction with the Higgs Field gives them their mass. In the same way, all the Strings are essentially massless and are all traveling with the speed of light. However, since there are smaller dimensions that are invisible on our scale, these strings travel through those dimensions and therefore appear to move slower through space, i.e., appear to have mass.

14.4: SUMMARY

Since it is believed that there are six dimensions curled upon themselves, it increases the types of vibrations in strings. This further increases the types of particles that possibly exist in the universe. Another interesting thing is, there are multiple ways in which six dimensions can curl up, but each universe has a specific way in which it is curled up to maintain the symmetries of spacetime. This means that the different ways in which these six dimensions curl up each corresponds to different universes with different types of particles.

Although it is unknown about the way in which the dimensions are curled up in our universe, carefully organizing the six-dimensions in a way such that they predict the particles present in our universe can be done to find it out. However, it is still unclear why do we have the particles of the Standard Model instead of infinite other possibilities. According to some speculations, the geometry of the universe might be varying over time, which means that the way the dimensions are arranged might be changing over a period.

But like every other hypothetical theory, this one too has a problem. Most of the concept of String Theory is based on the Supersymmetry of Fermions and Bosons. If it is so, then there are still many particles that are yet to be discovered. That said, this theory is one of the most promising models which has enabled us to study quantum gravity and black holes, and potentially described Axion as a particle of dark matter. This theory has also enabled us to understand the Standard Model in a much deeper way.

However, all we know till now is that String Theory is a speculative theory. It is almost impossible to test this theory experimentally since the strings themselves would be extremely tiny. Also, this isn't the only theory that tries to combine Quantum Mechanics with General Relativity. It is possible that this is only a hypothetical model which doesn't describe the fundamental nature of the universe. However, there is still a long way to go for scientists to conclude the true nature of reality and to conclusively define the true 'Theory of Everything'.

Bibliography

1. https://www.youtube.com/watch?v=XYcw8nV_GTs
2. https://www.youtube.com/watch?v=asEtNJ9sRcQ
3. https://www.youtube.com/watch?v=TDYex6VSd7o
4. https://www.youtube.com/watch?v=JP9KP-fwFhk&t=525s
5. https://www.youtube.com/watch?v=Iuv6hY6zsd0&t=11s
6. https://www.youtube.com/watch?v=h75DGO3GrF4
7. https://www.youtube.com/watch?v=ZuvK-od647c&list=WL&index=10
8. https://www.youtube.com/watch?v=JFozGfxmi8A&t=96s
9. https://www.youtube.com/watch?v=lQapfUcf4Do
10. https://www.youtube.com/watch?v=YstJxj30hzs&t=182s
11. https://www.youtube.com/watch?v=uZDhCW-PTRM
12. https://www.youtube.com/watch?v=a8FTr2qMutA
13. https://www.youtube.com/watch?v=bD2M7P6dTVA
14. https://www.youtube.com/watch?v=vruYFOlM1-Q&t=540s
15. https://www.youtube.com/watch?v=jHoEjvuPoB8&list=WL&index=3
16. https://www.youtube.com/watch?v=JhHMJCUmq28
17. https://www.youtube.com/watch?v=RCj_BJ6BddM&list=WL&index=12
18. https://www.youtube.com/watch?v=ATcrrzJFtBY&list=WL&index=6&t=753s
19. https://www.youtube.com/watch?v=FBeALt3rxEA
20. https://www.youtube.com/watch?v=hHTWBc14-mk

21. https://www.youtube.com/watch?v=PutOOpAkjQ4
22. https://www.youtube.com/watch?v=S3Wtat5QNUA&t=115s
23. https://www.youtube.com/watch?v=yuD34tEpRFw
24. https://www.youtube.com/watch?v=ZAf7FXih-Jc
25. https://www.youtube.com/watch?v=TI6sY0kCPpk&list=WL&index=5&t=3s
26. https://www.youtube.com/watch?v=Da-2h2B4faU&list=WL&index=2
27. https://www.youtube.com/watch?v=YNEBhwimJWs&t=616s

About The Author

Bhavya Bansal is currently studying in 10th-grade, at Sat Paul Mittal School in Ludhiana, Punjab. Bhavya loves to explore new things and has an analytical bend towards Science and Mathematics. He has got his name registered in the "India Book of Records 2018". Bhavya has won many National and International prizes in the field of Robotics. He has been invited as a Guest Speaker at many scientific meetings. He is excellent at academics and has many research papers to his credit.

Bhavya Bansal

9 798886 298864

Printed by Libri Plureos GmbH in Hamburg,
Germany